T0080961

INSIDE
BLUES
GUITAR

Publisher *David A. Lusterman*
Editor *Jeffrey Pepper Rodgers*
Managing Editor *Stacey Lynn*
Music Editor *Andrew DuBrock*
Designer *Barbara Gelfand*
Production *Susan Pinkerton*
Production Director *Ellen Richman*
Marketing *Jen Fujimoto*
Music Engraving *Andrew DuBrock*

Photographs: front cover, clockwise from top left, by Paul Luscher, Rory
Earnshaw, and Joe Alper (courtesy of Frank Driggs); title page, p. 76, and back
cover by Rory Earnshaw; pp. viii, 3, 4, 7, 9, 12, 16, 21, 23, 34, 42, 49, and 52
courtesy Frank Driggs; p. 14 by Tom Radcliffe/Point of View; pp. 24 and 41
courtesy Sears, Roebuck, and Co.; pp. 28 and 60 by Mark Weakley; p. 29 by
Paul Schraub; p. 32 by Suzanne Manchester/ELO Productions; p. 35 by
Russell Hibbard; p. 36 courtesy Deering Banjo Co.; p. 38 by Todd Wolfson;
p. 54 by Robert Tilling/International Guitar Seminars; p. 58 by Paul Luscher

Contents © 2001 Steve James

Printed in the United States of America
All rights reserved.
This book was produced by String Letter Publishing, Inc.
PO Box 767, San Anselmo, CA 94979-0767; (415) 485-6946;
www.stringletter.com

Library of Congress Cataloging-in-Publication Data

James, Steve, 1950-
  Inside blues guitar/by Steve James.
      p. cm. – (Acoustic guitar guides)
  ISBN 1-890490-36-9
1. Guitar–Instruction and study. 2. Guitar music (Blues)–History
and criticism. 3. Blues (Music)–Instruction and study. 1. Title. II.
Series.
  MT580 .J36 2001
  787.87'193'1643–dc21

                                        2001020864

String Letter Publishing

INSIDE BLUES GUITAR

STEVE JAMES

STRING LETTER PUBLISHING

CONTENTS

TECHNIQUES AND TUNINGS

PRACTICING AND PERFORMING

INTRODUCTION

More than a century after it first emerged from the rural South, blues music remains one of America's most vital musical legacies. New generations of fans discover the primal power of this music decade after decade, as new players—especially guitarists—continue to revisit and extend the tradition. Although interest in blues remains intense, knowledge of its roots is often sketchy, even among players. The intent of *Inside Blues Guitar* is to provide a concise, approachable guide to where the music came from, who its essential voices were, and what the techniques are that define it for the contemporary musician.

The 50 questions in this book are those most often asked by blues fans, particularly guitarists. Many were sent in over the course of the decade to *Acoustic Guitar* magazine, for which I am a contributing editor, by mail and through its Web site. Some were extrapolated from the articles, reviews, and columns I've contributed over the years, and others are paraphrases of queries I get often at guitar workshops, from fans at concerts, or from my own mailbox. All the questions and answers included here relate in some way to the blues as it's played on the acoustic guitar. It was our aim, however, to create a text that would be not only useful to the guitarist, but enjoyable and informative for any reader who likes blues music. Some of the questions are concise, and the answers are as informational as space allows. Others are more abstract—some even humorous—and I tried to answer them in kind.

If many of the references made here seem to relate to music of the 1920s and '30s, the reason is twofold: First, a tremendous body of acoustic guitar blues was recorded during that period, and the music is still popular and influential today. Second, after electric guitars were introduced in the '30s, most blues players started using them. Although many electric stylists draw heavily on the acoustic repertoire, the focus here is on blues specifically played on an acoustic guitar. Brief mention is made of guitarists such as Reverend Gary Davis, Blind Willie Johnson, and Merle Travis. Their work in the gospel and country fields is not to be overlooked by guitarists in any style, but it falls outside the strict classification of blues.

Appended to the main text is a discography that lists at least one available recording by almost every artist mentioned here. Also included is a bibliography. These titles are not only recommended reading; I used them as reference material during the preparation of this book.

Finally, I hope that this text affords some basic information, from blues origins to bottleneck slides to busking, and also expresses some of the very real enjoyment to be found listening to and playing acoustic blues.

STYLES AND STYLISTS

Since the 1700s the term has been used to describe a melancholy or depressed feeling. It has referred to a

What is the blues?

body of secular music, African-American in origin, that has expressed that feeling since before the turn of the last century. Since blues—the art form—places emphasis on individual experience, the blues means different things to different people. The sounds that Texas-born swing and bop guitar pioneer Charlie Christian described as blues might have been unrecognizable as such to rural bluesmen who preceded him by only a generation. Meanwhile, the music of "blue yodeler" Jimmie Rodgers and the archaic stylings of Mississippi John Hurt fall outside the frame of reference of many modern "blooze" fans who, in turn, boogie furiously to guitar sounds that would have earned a cautionary growl from Howlin' Wolf.

Musically speaking, especially for the guitarist, there are a few simple truths. First among these are the scalar intervals called *blue notes* that are a harmonic feature of all blues. They include the flatted or slurred third, fifth, and seventh degrees of the diatonic major scale. First, a major scale in the key of A has the notes shown on the next page (see also Musical Examples appendix).

A	B	C#	D	E	F#	G#
1	2	3	4	5	6	7

Add the flatted third and fifth and substitute the flatted seventh, and the scale takes on a blues tonality:

A	B	C	C#	D	E♭	E	F#	G
1	2	♭3	3	4	♭5	5	6	♭7

Elements of blues tonality as they relate to the guitar will be further discussed later in this book.

Almost all blues is played in duple meter—that is, measures composed of beats joined in multiples of two—and is usually expressed or written in 4/4 time. The most common lyric scheme involves two rhyming lines of four measures each:

> *I hate to see the evenin' sun go down . . .*
> *Makes me think I'm on my last go-round . . .*

Again, various verse structures and song forms will be detailed in subsequent pages.

With the blues, there's an exception to almost every rule. Lemon Jefferson, a prolific blues composer, certainly didn't feel limited by preconceived meter structures. Tommy Johnson and Charley Patton, two Delta legends whose work defines the genre, often sang verses that didn't rhyme. The libidinous "hokum" blues of guitar wizards like Tampa Red and Blind Blake don't express sadness . . . they're funny. Even when a singer claims he's "got the blues" because he drank up his paycheck or got into it with his girlfriend, it's another emotional world from that of the man who wonders aloud if he'll be released from a prison chain gang before he dies.

Another gray area surrounds the very origins of the blues.

When and where did people start playing and singing blues?

The simple answer is that nobody knows. Although other forms of African-American music such as minstrelsy and jubilee singing have documented origins traceable to the early 19th century, the people who first sang and played the blues remain nameless. Some informants have recalled hearing the blues as early as the 1880s, and it was common throughout the South by the first decade of the 1900s.

Certainly, the development of blues guitar style was abetted by the availability of cheap mail-order instruments, starting in the 1890s; but just how the styles spread is also something of a mystery. Spread they did, though. W.C. Handy first heard blues guitar played by a mystery slide man in Mississippi in 1903. Reverend Gary Davis' initial experience was in South Carolina the following year, and there have been concurrent remembrances by musicians from Kentucky to Texas.

Charley Patton, born in 1887, was one of the most powerful early voices of the blues.

Although the blues would soon dominate the sound of American popular music and become largely the medium of urban professionals, its origins were definitely rural.

Categorizing styles of blues isn't a simple undertaking—but certain classifications have come into use among scholars, collectors, and musicians. One of the most general of these is country blues. Perhaps the best way to briefly describe it is to compare the work of two popular early blues artists.

How would you describe "country blues"?

In 1920, when Mamie Smith recorded her "Crazy Blues" (touted as the first recorded performance in the genre) at OKeh Records' New York studio, she had been a professional theater and cabaret entertainer for nearly 25 years. The Cincinnati-born chanteuse was accompanied by the Jazz Hounds, a group of trained musicians led by clarinetist/composer Perry Bradford. Smith's seasoned voice and

Georgia guitarist Willie McTell played blues on a 12-string guitar better than anyone.

stage diction were complemented by a complex band arrangement. The hugely popular record defined a style now referred to as classic blues and was sung by stage veterans such as Gertrude "Ma" Rainey and Bessie Smith.

Six years later, Lemon Jefferson entered the Paramount recording facility in Chicago for his debut—"Long Lonesome Blues." The singer, blind since birth in rural east Texas, had absorbed traditional folk music and spirituals from his family and neighbors. By ear, he developed a prodigious and personal guitar and vocal style that he plied for tips at farm socials, on small-town street corners, and, finally, in the area of Dallas called Deep Ellum where he first appeared around 1914. Jefferson's powerful, nasal singing sounded almost like a field holler. His lyrics, full of down-home slang and symbolism, were delivered with a distinct Texas drawl and punctuated by improvised guitar phrases that stretched the meter between sung lines with fingerpicked cross-rhythms, walking bass lines, and sustained blue notes. The hugely popular record defined a style now referred to as *country blues.* With song forms drawn from traditional themes and the singers' own experience, it was performed by regional practitioners like Charley Patton and Willie McTell.

Although country blues has been played on harmonica and piano, and by string and jug bands, its principal instrumental voice is that of the guitar. The recorded repertoire includes some of the most unique and influential acoustic guitar performances in the known history of folk music.

South of Memphis, the Mississippi River and its tributaries have created a broad floodplain that covers the northwestern part of the state of Mississippi and contiguous eastern Arkansas. This is the Delta—board flat from the river east to the Tallahatchie Ridge and south to the bluffs at Vicksburg.

In the 19th century, as this fertile land was cleared for cultivation, the owners of what were to become giant cotton plantations began building earthen levees to control the Mississippi's savage seasonal floods. By 1900, the plantations were multithousand-acre fiefdoms with their own stores, post offices, and cotton gins. The land was worked by black laborers who farmed parcels in return for housing and credit against a share of what they grew. The levees, now bigger than the Great Wall of China, were maintained by contractors who housed their "skinners"—black men renowned for their skill handling teams of draft mules—in remote tent villages called levee camps. It was among these sharecroppers and muleskinners that some of the first blues was played and sung.

In the late 1920s, when record company scouts first turned their attention to the Delta, they found some of the greatest talents in early recorded blues. There were originators like Tommy Johnson and the astounding Charley Patton. Patton was kingpin of a group of bluesmen including the brilliant guitarist Willie Brown and Son House, whose explosive intensity set a mark for younger players like Robert Johnson and Muddy Waters. The core Delta repertoire included variations on themes like "Roll and Tumble" and "Pony Blues," shaped by each artist into a unique statement. The guitar playing was distinguished by strong picked and slapped bass figures underpinning bluesy modal riffs; Delta players also made frequent use of open tunings and bottleneck slide guitar.

Although the early Delta bluesmen generally stuck close to home, their creative progeny certainly didn't; and here lies much of the importance of the Delta sound in modern music. Robert Johnson died before his talents were widely recognized, but his Delta contemporaries—Elmore James, Howlin' Wolf, and Muddy Waters—lived to shape the music of the Delta into a new sound that ultimately entered the realm of popular music.

Like Delta blues, these are references to older blues styles that developed in different areas of the South and are typified by the music of specific players from those regions.

In Texas, as in Mississippi, blues was being played by the turn of the last century. An independent republic in 1836, Texas gained statehood in 1845 and saw a significant influx of population from the Deep South that continued in the decades after the Civil War. Intensive cultivation of cotton and sugar cane in the "bottoms" adjacent to the Brazos and Trinity rivers in the eastern part of the state called for the construction of levees, while a growing timber industry based in the trackless Big Thicket gave rise to isolated logging camps with quarters, commissaries, and wide-open "barrelhouses" maintained for the black labor force. The area was another hotbed of early blues—from the aggressive piano style called "fast Texas" to the melismatic guitar phrases that answered sung lines in tunes like "Black Gal" and "Which Way Does the Red River Run?" During the early 1900s, as railroads criss-crossed the state, and boll weevils savaged the cotton crop, the Texas population became more urban, and so did its blues music. By the recording era of the 1920s, cities such as Dallas, Houston, Galveston, and San Antonio all had active music scenes with a diverse palette of blues sounds. Notable among the Texas guitarists were Henry "Ragtime" Thomas, Funny Paper Smith, Willard "Ramblin'" Thomas, Little Hat Jones, and, of course, Lemon Jefferson.

Another urban magnet for rural musicians was Atlanta, Georgia, where blues recording began in 1926 and '27 when Joshua "Peg Leg" Howell and Blind Willie McTell made sides for the Victor label. Atlanta lies near the southern extremity of the so-called Piedmont, which covers the foothills of the Appalachians from Georgia north through the Carolinas. The area was home to a remarkable group of guitarists including Willie Walker and Blind Boy Fuller. The guitar style of this cotton, corn, and tobacco country is associated with fleet, melodic blues and ragtime, as was the neighboring southeastern seaboard home of Blind Blake.

Once again, you can only go so far with these modern classifications. Most of what we know about early blues guitar styles is gleaned from recorded performances, and it's common knowledge that some of the great players from various regions were seldom or never recorded. In addition, by the early '20s, many of the subsequently recorded masters—Blake and Jefferson for example—had traveled widely, picking up and dropping off elements of style wherever they went. Jefferson's "One Dime Blues," waxed in '27, is also a staple in the Piedmont repertoire. Did he learn it on one of his documented trips to the Carolinas? Did they learn it from him? Or was the parent piece, "Make Me a Pallet on Your Floor," known to an even earlier generation of musicians throughout the South? Go figure.

Howlin' Wolf (shown here at Silvio's in Chicago in the 1960s) and other Chicago-based musicians plugged in the music of the Delta and laid the foundation for rock 'n' roll.

Remember also that all great musical performances, especially blues, reflect the world view of an individual creative artist. Simply calling Lemon Jefferson a "Texas bluesman" is like calling Johann Sebastian Bach a "German organist"—it only tells part of a larger story.

Most blues fans think immediately of the ensembles of Muddy Waters, Howlin' Wolf, and Elmore James, who recorded popular blues for Chess and other Chicago-based labels in the 1950s. The postwar Chicago sound, with heavily amplified guitar and harmonica sorties driven by muscular, jazz-tinged drumming, was derived in no small part from the music of the Delta—and was a direct influence on the rock styles that followed.

What differentiates Chicago blues from other styles?

Chicago, however, had been a blues epicenter since the early 20th century, when over a million rural southerners migrated to northern cities. In the early '20s it was home to a legion of jazz and blues groundbreakers, including guitarists Lonnie Johnson and Blind Blake.

It was the headquarters of Paramount Records—a leader in blues recording—and its active performing and recording scene prompted frequent visits by a host of blues icons. African-American culture in the Windy City was further promulgated by the *Chicago Defender,* America's first black-owned newspaper. It extolled the advantages of urban life in the North and was widely distributed in the South, further prompting rural blacks to leave for the big city.

The hybrid, experimental nature of Chicago blues of the '50s was also prevalent in its earlier incarnation. Regional and individual styles melded as players from "back home" arrived, ready to jam and exchange ideas. The jazz, country, boogie-woogie, and popular music that also proliferated richened the mix.

The down-home-meets-uptown ethos prevailed during the Depression, when the mantle of fallen recording giants Paramount and Columbia was assumed by new labels like Decca, Bluebird, and ARC/Vocalion. In this environment, singer/guitarists Big Bill Broonzy, Tampa Red, Bumble Bee Slim, Memphis Minnie, Yank Rachell, Big Joe Williams, and others flourished creatively. Along with harmonica ace John Lee "Sonny Boy" Williamson and a number of other writers and instrumentalists, they experimented with electric instruments and various group formats, recording songs like "Good Morning Little Schoolgirl" and "Baby, Please Don't Go," which were basic to the Chicago sound of the postwar era.

Who are the essential early blues guitarists?

Early recorded blues, like the music of today, had its hitmakers. Their songs and styles were big with the public, and they strongly influenced their contemporaries, as well as generations to come. Among them were not a few guitarists . . . so let's start our "gimme list" with five string marvels who moved some units back in the 1920s.

We've already mentioned Lemon Jefferson. His dense, varied guitar style defies duplication, but many of his devices were copied by other guitarists. Jefferson's music was popular among white and black listeners alike; you can even hear elements of his style in the playing of proto-country star Jimmie Rodgers. "I was crazy about him . . . My whole family was crazy about him!" said T-Bone Walker, recalling the boyish excitement he felt when the blind recording star visited his Dallas neighborhood.

A contemporary of Jefferson's (they debuted on disc in 1926) was Lonnie Johnson from New Orleans. No "country" bluesman this; he played violin and banjo in the dance and stage orchestras of Fate Marable and Will Marion Cook before he began playing blues on the guitar. His sophistication was evident on "Mr. Johnson's Blues" and a spate of recordings to follow—the intricate chord vamps that accompanied his vocals were punctuated by agile single-string runs and buttery bent notes. Johnson's career as a bluesman—with forays into jazz and R&B—continued until his death in 1972.

Then (sigh) there's Blind Blake . . . "Blake played so much guitar that I started to put the whole mess down and forget it,"

Lonnie Johnson brought an urban sophistication not only to blues but to jazz and R&B in his five-decade career.

Big Bill Broonzy told Alan Lomax of their first meeting. Like Jefferson and Johnson, Blake made dozens of solo acoustic recordings. His initial outing for Paramount in '26 paired the languid "Early Morning Blues" with "West Coast Blues." Blake's guitaristic trump card, "West Coast Blues" is a fast "piano-sounding" blues-rag whose drive and complexity was, and still is, a challenge for the guitar fingerstylist. (Also an important American symbolist philosopher, Blake was among the first to explore the true meaning of "diddie-wah-diddie.")

The runaway blues hit of 1928 was the naughty "Tight Like That." It defined the "hokum" style and featured the slide guitar of Hudson Whitaker—better known as Tampa Red. The fluid bottleneck style of this freckled fretster did a lot to rehabilitate the technique (formerly considered old-fashioned) among a younger generation of musicians. Slide masters Robert Nighthawk, Elmore James, and Earl Hooker were among many fond of quoting Red's legato lines.

On the heels of "Tight Like That" came the brooding "How Long, How Long Blues." Leroy Carr's vocal and piano work was colored a deeper blue by the textured guitar fills of South Carolinian Francis "Scrapper" Blackwell. (Blackwell's own "Kokomo Blues" was later adapted as the too-familiar "Sweet Home Chicago.") Together, Carr and Blackwell personified a sense of rocking, urban "cool" that would become pervasive in the blues, and their first hit was basic repertoire for many young musicians doing their journey work at the time, including Robert Johnson and Muddy Waters.

There are five great guitar players who had a significant effect on the way people played back then—and on the way we play now. Listen to their music and, if you're like me, you'll want to hear some more.

Who are some of the other musicians you would place in the "required listening" category?

Two standouts are the previously mentioned Charley Patton and Blind Willie McTell. Although during their lives their discs weren't accorded the popularity of those made by Jefferson or Blake, both were prolific in the studio. Patton and McTell were consummate stylists, defining the music of their time and place while also creating a sound of their own, and both were absolutely brilliant guitarists.

Patton's primacy in the Delta, where he was born in 1887, is evinced by the awed respect he engendered in great bluesmen like Howlin' Wolf and Bukka White (neither given to hyperbole). Patton didn't record until 1929 and died in 1934, but he waxed more than 55 titles in that short period, including folk songs and spirituals along with a variety of blues. Patton's gruff lyricism dealt with everything from erotic metaphor to the Mississippi flood of 1927 and was accompanied by guitar parts that ranged from melancholic slide to pounding chord vamps.

Willie McTell's repertoire, like Patton's, was not limited to the blues, but nobody ever played the blues better on the 12-string guitar. His recording career stretched from 1927 to 1956 and, as can be guessed, his output was prodigious—you can literally spend a whole day listening to this Georgia genius. In addition to his technical prowess, McTell had a real songwriter's gift, evidenced by often-covered titles like "Statesboro Blues" and "Broke Down Engine." He customarily set his compositions to beautiful arrangements, and his fluency in a number of tunings and styles—from slide to ragtime—makes his work of special interest to the guitarist.

Given that the bulk of blues recordings of the '20s and '30s were made by commercial labels whose principal concern was the bottom line rather than folklore, the number and variety of styles and artists that were cataloged is phenomenal. A (very) short list of my top picks would include the Beale Street Sheiks—Frank Stokes and Dan Sane. Stokes' songbag included blues and pre-blues themes; each one was shored up by the Sheiks' signature synchro-mesh duet guitar sound. Another top-drawer talent from Memphis is Walter "Furry" Lewis, whose blues-ballad "Kassie Jones" is a classic. Lewis didn't play a lot of notes, but he owned every note he played. In contrast, Armenter Chatmon (aka Bo Carter) did play a lot of notes. His skill as a guitarist is often overshadowed by his uncanny ability to create sexual imagery out of anything from a cigarette to a shoe, but the licks this Mississippian coaxed out of his National are a unique sound in blues. While Carter recorded a staggering 112 titles, Garfield Akers only cut three . . . but if he'd never done anything but the pulsing "Dough Roller," it would have been enough for me. I once listened to this drop-dead minimalist masterpiece 20 times in succession.

Beware of blues myopia, however. A lot of great bluesy guitar playing can be heard on records classified in the "country" genre, from Sam McGee to Harvey and Copeland to Merle Travis. Also, the so-called devil's box made frequent appearances in church. The "holy blues" of Reverend Gary Davis is cited as an influence by just about every roots-revival fingerstylist performing today. Texas guitar evangelist Blind Willie Johnson is simply one of the best slide players ever recorded. If you aspire to bottleneck virtuosity and haven't heard the grave music of this sightless saint, you're missing the boat.

Just as most of the classic blues singers were women, early blues guitar style was largely a man's game. The idiom did have its queen though. Lizzie Douglas started her musical career long before she recorded her 1929 hit "Bumble Bee" under the name Memphis Minnie;

All these people are men! Aren't there any notable women guitarists in early blues?

but when this gold-toothed Louisiana country girl chanted, "He got all the

Memphis Minnie, shown here in 1946, was a groundbreaker in both acoustic and electric blues guitar styles.

stinger I need," and backed up the image with some of the toughest blues guitar to date, she made a place for herself among Chicago's blues elite. She "played like a man," opined Big Bill Broonzy, one of many who felt the heat in guitar throw-downs with Ms. Douglas. Memphis Minnie's career as a soloist and session player continued into the '50s. She was one of the pioneers of electric blues guitar and is recognized as an early architect of the postwar Chicago sound.

Isolated appearances on record by guitar-playing blueswomen like Geechie Wiley, and the bluesy guitar licks of Rosetta Tharpe and other female gospel singers, suggest that more women have played blues guitar than recorded it. There's further evidence that women who never made it to the studio were influential in the development of early blues guitar style. Here are two examples.

Savannah Weaver was the mother of James "Curley" Weaver, whose solo recordings and duets with Willie McTell are definitive. Curley's primary guitar influence was his mom. Savannah also taught the neighbor kids, "Barbecue Bob" Hicks and his brother "Laughing Charlie" Lincoln, who, along with McTell and Weaver, were the apogee of early recorded Georgia country blues.

The real mystery girl is Delta singer/guitarist Josie Bush. She was remembered well by area musicians like Mott Willis, who described her playing in superlative terms. Bush played with (and has been romantically linked to) Willie Brown, who was touted as the "best guitar player in the Delta." At least one of her themes, "Riverside Blues," was adapted by a number of players, becoming something of a Delta standard.

Is it possible that the stereotype of the "chick" singer and the guitar-slinging "dude" is just one more rock retention from early blues? As the old gospel song says: "The half ain't never been told."

All these people are dead! Is there a contemporary acoustic blues scene?

Well, yeah, there certainly is. The conditions that spawned the blues are (thankfully) history, but the sound of primal blues guitar remains. The way these styles and repertoire have been disseminated among musicians around the world is a bit of social history in itself, as is the remarkable way that the early sounds have woven themselves into the fabric of contemporary "alternative" and popular music.

The term *race records* as applied to African-American roots music in the 1920s tells a lot about the audience at the time, and even more about the marketing philosophy of the record labels. Even as musicians relocated to northern cities, they found audiences much like themselves—recent arrivals from the South—and their music was presented accordingly. The "race" ethic persisted into the 1930s. Then materials shortages brought on by World War II and a recording ban initiated by the musicians union in 1942 brought a veritable halt to commercial recording activities. It was in the years during and after the war that the real shift occurred in the way acoustic blues was marketed and heard.

Through the '40s and '50s, artists like Leadbelly, Big Bill Broonzy, Brownie McGhee, and Josh White found a new audience, mostly urban and almost entirely white, of folk-music aficionados. These performers were able to adapt their styles and repertoire to the new market as their music became available on labels like Decca or the tiny specialty outfits Musicraft and Asch. As these progenitors of the "authentic" folk blues sound toured in the States and abroad, they were inevitably heard by a new generation of guitarists. Once again, the sound of acoustic blues influenced the way people played, from the British skiffle movement to American popular folk music. For every raft of hootennanophiles, there was a guitarist or two who

Piedmont bluesman John Jackson has been sharing his down-home style for more than 60 years. Here he holds a cutaway resonator guitar made by Ron Phillips.

crouched over Harry Smith's *Anthology of American Folk Music* asking themselves not "Is this one we can all sing?" but "What the hell tuning is he in?"

By the time I ponied up for a brand-new 1964 Gibson, the musical language of the folkie was being further augmented by "discoveries" like Mississippi John Hurt. It still strains my retrospective credulity to recall a 24-hour period at the 1966 Newport Folk Festival that included sets by Son House, Skip James, Lightnin' Hopkins, and Bukka White along with Ed Young's Mississippi Fife and Drum Band and Howlin' Wolf. Also on the bill was the Jim Kweskin Jug Band, an aggregate emblematic of the roots revival whose vanguard included John Hammond and Dave Van Ronk. Purists railed because they were white and looked more like they'd been to Princeton than prison. Kids like me loved them because they played great and had cool shoes. . . . Anyway, there they were.

And here we are. I recently heard an installment of the popular broadcast *A Prairie Home Companion* that featured the voice and guitar of Geoff Muldaur, a founding member of the Kweskin band, and reflected on the longevity and pliancy of the music. I've never been sure if the word *revival* accurately describes the convoluted journey that American roots music has taken, but if anything indeed was revived, it sure as hell stayed that way.

Trying to make a comprehensible, let alone comprehensive, lexicon of artists presently recording and performing who have incorporated the acoustic blues sound into their music is daunting. Even the short list, one of people whose paths I've crossed on the road over the last year, was approaching 50 names before I quit—knowing that I'd just leave somebody out. Quite a number of players are mentioned in context through the pages that follow, but the story doesn't end there.

While I was writing this, I got a call from the Centrum organization in Port Townsend, Washington, which sponsors an annual series of concerts and workshops called Country Blues Week. I'll be happy to be on the program again this year, not only because the senior instructor/performers in the guitar department will be John Jackson and John Cephas, with their cumulative 130 years of playing experience, or because the rest of the staff will be new and old friends with songs to play and lies to tell. I'm looking forward to meeting the 150-plus participants who'll show up from all over the country and the world—little kids barely bigger than the guitars they're toting, young dudes and dudettes who think they want my job, and older folks who always wanted to play like this . . . and finally found time to learn.

WORDS AND MUSIC

A bar across the musical staff marks a measure, and each measure has a specific number of beats. Blues

What is a 12-bar blues?

music is usually expressed in 4/4 time—that is, in measures containing four beats each (each beat given the value of a quarter note). So a 12-bar blues verse is one composed of 12 four-beat measures.

The typical way to construct a lyric for a 12-bar blues is to sing a line of four measures in length, repeat that line, and finish the verse by singing another four-measure line that rhymes with the first. A basic instrumental accompaniment can be played using the I (tonic), IV (subdominant), and V (dominant) chords—that is, the chords built around the first, fourth, and fifth degrees of the scale that corresponds to the key of the song. For instance, in the key of A, the I chord is A, the IV is D, and the V is E. A 12-bar progression in A might look like the example at right. A slightly more complex version of this progression, with melody and lyrics, is included in the appendix. This is the most commonly used blues form, but it's by no means the only one.

A 12-bar blues in A. The ∠ symbol means repeat the chord from the previous measure.

17

"All blues sounds the same to me . . ." some people will say. A whole set of 12-bar blues can get a little monochromatic, it's true, but the acoustic blues bag offers a number of other bar structures and chord progressions. The eight-bar blues form was and is commonly used; the ubiquitous "Sitting on Top of the World" is one good example (see appendix). Variations on this melody and structure have been used many times, and it's still a good vehicle for the songwriter. Note the similarities between this song and other blues standards such as "Trouble in Mind." Another common eight-bar theme is typified by the song "Key to the Highway."

A blues song that has also become a country and bluegrass favorite is "Nine Pound Hammer," which couples an eight-bar verse with an eight-bar chorus to create a song with a 16-bar structure. Another 16-bar theme is the old blues number "Make Me a Pallet on Your Floor."

Pieces like "Milk Cow Blues," often interpreted by western swingers, join 12- and 16-bar verses; and the suggestive "Dirty Dozens" has an open-ended structure that allows the singer to expand on the basic 16-bar form as long as he or she can conjure up off-color metaphors. (Bottleneck bad boy Kokomo Arnold has an especially pungent version.)

Skip James' anthem "Devil Got My Woman" is based on a 12-bar form, but the chord accompaniment simply alternates from I to V, leaving out the IV chord entirely. The archaic classic "Catfish Blues," adapted by James along with Robert Petway, Muddy Waters, and a host of others, is a modal construction: it has no chord changes at all. The more blues you listen to, the more structural diversity you'll hear.

Are there some basic blues rhythms?

As we've seen, blues music is usually expressed in 4/4 time, so the basic count is: 1, 2, 3, 4. In blues, the second and fourth beats are often emphasized—that is, played louder than the first and third. These accented beats are called the *backbeats*. Whether you're playing a simple strum pattern or the *boom chang* of alternating-bass–style fingerpicking, a basic rhythm figure would have bass notes on beats 1 and 3 and accented chords on beats 2 and 4 (see appendix for this and other rhythm examples).

A single beat can be divided by odd or even increments—basically by two or three. Double up on the rhythm by playing two strums per beat or, if you're fingerpicking, by interjecting a finger upstroke between two downstrokes of your thumb: 1 and 2 and 3 and 4 and.

Another rhythm pattern often used in slow to medium tempo blues involves superimposing a triplet (1-and-a) over each beat in a 4/4 measure. (Sometimes you will see songs using this pattern notated in 12/8 instead of 4/4 time, but the feel is the same.)

If you're fingerpicking, play the "on" beats with downstrokes of your thumb and the fast triplets with upstrokes of your fingers. Sometimes referred to as playing "six over two," this is an approach used, for instance, by Memphis Minnie on her "Bumble Bee" and by Big Bill Broonzy on his various renditions of the "Key to the Highway" theme.

Syncopation is the basic rhythmic syntax in the language of ragtime, jazz, and blues. It's a rhythmic device that's usually achieved by sustaining a tone through a beat stronger than the one on which it began. The accent shifts because the normally "weak" tone absorbs the accent of the beat through which it's held. Try counting out the example at right, and note how many of the underlined accents fall on the *and* beats.

1	and	2	and	3	and	4	and

1	and	2	and	3	and	4	and

A syncopated rhythm, with accents falling on the underlined beats.

One kind of syncopation, sometimes called a *shuffle* in blues, can be played by accenting the volume of a normally "weak" beat, like the *and* after 3 and 4. These subtle shifts in accent within the framework of a steady beat are the basis of that hard-to-define quality called *swing* that is common to blues performance.

What is a turnaround?

The expression is used to describe a harmonic figure generally used at the end of a verse to anticipate the beginning of the next verse. A simple turnaround is done by restating the dominant (V) chord in the last measure. On page 20 is a 12-bar blues progression in A with a turnaround to the V—the final E chord that leads back into the A.

A 12-bar blues with a turnaround.

In the appendix, you can see this turnaround written out, as well as a few variations that add in some other chords for color. Plus I've written out the hands-down favorite turnaround at guitar workshops—Robert Johnson used it all the time—which involves a descending bass line in A on the fourth string played over a repeated high A note on the first string, leading into a turnaround on the E (V) chord.

Turnarounds are fun and useful, but not necessary to complete a blues verse. Notice that they're largely absent in older country blues song forms.

How do you write original songs and arrangements in a "traditional" blues style?

Here's some good advice from the man who wrote "Key to the Highway":

Now let me tell you about how I make my blues. Soon as something jump up in my mind, I put it right down. You got to put down that verse that comes to you first, when it comes to you, and let that take effect on you first; then the others will come with the feeling.

—Big Bill Broonzy, from an interview with Alan Lomax

A good blues song, like any other, creates a picture in the mind of the listener . . . it tells a story. What makes the blues form such an effective vehicle is the same thing that can make a good blues verse hard to write—its simplicity. Lyrically, combining an abstract or open image with a concrete one is a writing technique often used in blues that allows the listener to interpret their own experience into the song:

I can feel the wind is risin' . . . leaves tremblin' on the trees
I need my li'l sweet rider . . . to keep me company
—Robert Johnson

Used in the blues context, a plain image like that of falling rain or a setting sun can be used to deepen the descriptive or emotional quality of a line of verse.

Both musically and lyrically, there are quite a number of lines or themes that have been used repeatedly by blues composers; and it's perfectly all right to adapt them again, but try to avoid cliches. Maybe you've seen that tiresome piece of Internet spam that professes to be a guide to the blues and suggests that a good blues song starts with the line: "My baby done left me." I don't know about you, but I can't get much out of a guy who caterwauls "My baby done left me and put my clothes outdoors" when she's actually back at the condo, microwaving a Guiltless Gourmet veggie casserole and running his tennis outfit through the washer-dryer.

Ask ten songwriters how they go about composing a song . . . and you'll hear some really weird stuff! I'm a riff writer, mostly—one of those who likes to start with an idea or a hook line (lyric and melody) and then go for that mood on the guitar. Once I've got a basic arrangement, the rest of the song usually writes itself.

Big Bill Broonzy, author of the blues staple "Key to the Highway," advises writers to follow the feeling of their first idea.

I've written and recorded a number of blues and have had enough covers by other artists to make me like my mailbox. But I don't like to feel limited by the blues genre or by a preconception of what sounds "traditional" or "authentic."

A lot of Charley's words . . . you can be sitting right under him, you can't hardly understand him.
> —Son House on Patton, from an interview with John Fahey

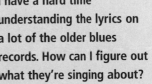

I have a hard time understanding the lyrics on a lot of the older blues records. How can I figure out what they're singing about?

A lot of early country blues singers had thick accents and rough voices and sang obscure place names and dialect expressions no longer in common use. This can make blues lyrics hard for people who speak conventional English to decipher. Recently, in a bar in Budapest, I was asked by a group of musicians to explain the meaning of the phrase: "She th'owed mah clo'se ow-doze." Their inability to reconcile the pronunciation with their book-learned English was complicated by the fact that they were unfamiliar with the convention of depositing garments in the yard.

Dialect problems are compounded by the reality that it was a common practice among early blues record producers to supply their artists with a few drinks before a session to loosen them up. You can hear numerous instances on old blues records where the singers are obviously hammered, which doesn't make them any easier to understand. If you're having difficulties along this line, ask your drunk friends from the South to help you; but if you don't already know such people, don't seek them out. Most blues tablature books have pretty accurate transcriptions of the song lyrics. There are even some good lyric compilations; I recommend *The Country Blues Songbook,* by Stephen Calt (Oak Publications).

Another factor in the comprehensibility of blues lyrics (and music for that matter) is the quality of the recordings themselves. Many reissues have been mastered directly from old 78-rpm discs. When these have been played over and over, there is invariably a lot of surface hiss, along with clicks and pops from scratches. This is coupled with the unfortunate fact that many of these records were poorly made to begin with. Modern mastering technology has done a lot to clean up some of the old stuff, but there are instances where there's only one known copy of a disc, and it's beat. In cases like this, you just have to figure out which you like to do more—listen to high-fidelity sound recordings, or listen to Son House.

What exactly happens when you get your "ashes hauled" or your "broom dusted"? Is your mojo really connected to your hand?

The use of metaphor and double entendre to describe actions and things has always been common in blues lyrics. Sexual wordplay became especially popular during the early days of recording when the public wanted racy songs but the performers were enjoined from using graphic language in the studio. The sex/work metaphor is prevalent; the most common usage is a reference to "rolling." Literally, "rolling" is moving freight or materials from one place to another. It's repetitive, time-consuming work that requires strength

and endurance to do well. Get it? Hauling ashes is what you do after cleaning out a stove or hearth prior to lighting the fire. This suggestive image was used by Sleepy John Estes when he sang, "You may starch my jumper / Hang it upside your wall / You know by that, baby / I need my ashes hauled."

Broom dusting is another metaphor entirely, and a poignant one. It refers to sweeping out a domicile before vacating it. (Landlords often ask departing tenants to leave the premises "broom clean.") The lyric, originally recorded by Kokomo Arnold, was modified by Robert Johnson, who sang, "I'm getting up in the morning / I believe I'll dust my broom . . . / The black man you been loving / Girlfriend, can have my room." The "mojo" Muddy Waters sang about is an object that brings the bearer luck or power. These fetishes take many forms, a common one being that of a hand. Belief in the power of a hand-shaped charm to repel misfortune is ancient and transcultural. My mother inherited such a charm from her grandmother and hung it over my crib.

Pianist/vocalist Leroy Carr and guitarist Scrapper Blackwell, shown here in 1934, introduced the brooding "How Long, How Long Blues" to the repertoire.

Another palmate object with special properties is the root of the mandrake plant. Long used to make a narcotic potion, it was, in medieval times, ascribed such power that a person who pulled it from the ground could go mad. Hence, mandrake was harvested by specially trained dogs who were tied to the stem of the plant and called from a distance. While some have likened this sorcerer's root to a hand, it is more often compared to a human form, with the stem as the head and the roots issuing from a central body like arms and legs. In parlance, this potent little fellow is called High John the Conqueror Root—or, simply, John the Conqueroo—and can be used in the preparation of a powerful mojo.

By the way, mojos and similar charms are still being made and can be purchased if one knows where to look. I've been advised that they can be valuable if used properly, but in the hands of the frivolous or merely curious, they can be downright dangerous. Superstition? Maybe so, but it's probably better to spend the money on blues records.

$4.00 Monthly

$5.50 Monthly

Two-In-One Combinations
All Can Be Played Either Regular (Spanish) or Hawaiian Style

WE PAY THE POSTAGE

When Ordering on Easy Payments, Use Time Payment Order Blank in Back of Catalog.

5 MINUTE HAWAIIAN GUITAR

Artist

...lieve this is as fine and construc... is possible to buy ...oney. Back and sides ...koa wood imported ...m the Hawaiian ...Selected close grained ...op is beautifully in genuine mother-of-...ound top edge and ...all edges bound with white and ...shell celluloid. Stripe inlay on ...ck of genuine mahogany with rose-...eer headpiece inlaid with a pearl ...Oval fingerboard trimmed with ...hell celluloid and inlaid with pearl ...ornaments. Nickel plated patent ...ared to 12 to 1 ratio with ivoroid ...This guitar is of the special hand-...struction, and is fitted with the ...re to insure excellent .one quality. ...shed and polished finish. Two in-...books, three picks, a steel bar and ...nut for Hawaiian playing included.

8¼—We Pay $24.50
ayment Price, $5.00 down; $4.00 ....$27.25
9¼—Same, but Grand $28.45
ayment Price, $5.00 down; $4.00 ....$31.50

Trio

The very n... This instrume... carrying pow... used in conce... air playing great deal of ... Also suitable ...the volume d... sweet tone qu... tone, which i... ficed for vol...struments, i... by the metal diaphragm ...inner frame. This diaph... after those used in the la... graph reproducers. Body ...heavy construction, will s... of abuse. Finished in pol...Decalcomanias of various ...the top and back. Brass ...piece and patent heads g... ratio. A combination o... tone and volume. A thre... case, keratol (imitation ... and flannel lined, is incl... instruction books, steel ba... and three picks for playin... either regular (Spanish) o...

We Pay the Postage.
12T230¼............
Time Payment Price,
$5.50 a month.............

The Waikiki

Beautiful scenes of Hawaii, reproduced in nine colors, ornament the front and both sides of this standard size guitar. Natural finish spruce top trimmend with genuine wood block colored purfling of neat design, with white celluloid binding around edge and soundhole. Neck of hardwood with the pearlette fingerboard accurately fretted, and with 3 inlaid position dots. Pearlette headpiece and brass patent heads geared to 12 to 1 ratio. Body figured birch in imitation mahogany. Ebonized pin bridge. Two instruction books, three picks, steel bar and adjustable nut for playing Hawaiian style included. We Pay the Postage.

12T208¼
$9.45

12T207¼
As above but with ebonized fingerboard.
$8.25

The Entertainer
Genuine Mahogany

Here is an unusual value in a standard size guitar of genuine mahogany construction throughout. You will marvel at its fine appearance, neat construction and perfect design. You will be delighted with its wonderful tone qualities. A two-in-one Supertone Guitar with case and all accessories at this amazingly low price, represents a value we believe to be without equal anywhere. Mahogany neck has veneered headpiece; heavy ebonized fingerboard accurately fretted and with three pearl position dots. The top edge and sound-hole are inlaid with square cut colored wood block purfling, and trimmed with black and white striped celluloid. Extra heavy nickel plated brass tailpiece. Brass patent heads geared to 12 to 1 ratio and ebonized bridge. Finished in semi-gloss natural color. Outfit includes a "Biltwell" canvas case, fingerboard chart and two instruction books; also steel bar, adjustable nut and three picks for playing Hawaiian style. We Pay the Postage.

12T210¼ **$9.98**

$9.98 Postpaid

Learn to Play!

Do not fail to take advantage of the correspondence lessons by William Foden, the famous guitarist, or K. M. Baxter, the noted Hawaiian guitar player. Please mention on order for which course you want the lessons. See Page 721 for complete information.

Bradley Kincaid "Houn' Dog" Guitar

This is the guitar that the well know... radio artist, Bradley Kincaid, uses a... which he has named the "Houn' Dog" Guitar. Brad-ley will help you to learn his favorite selections, which he plays over the radio, as he has agreed to give one of his books with every "Houn' Dog" Guitar purchased. Body of figured mahogany with clear spruce top in natural finish. Top decorated with decalcomania of a mountain scene and "Houn' Dog," with Bradley Kincaid's signature. Top edge and soundhole trimmed with wood block colored purfling, and bound with white celluloid. Neck of mahogany with ebonized fingerboard, brass patent heads. Standard size. Bradley Kincaid's book of "Favorite Mountain Ballads and Old Time Songs," a five-minute instruction book and pick included. Postpaid.

BRADLEY KINCAID

12T411¼
$9.50

12T4432 — Steel bar, adjustable nut, two picks and instruction book for playing above guitar in Hawaiian style. Postpaid. 40c

The Handkraft

One of our very best guitars. Fine mahogany instrument made with a maximum of skilled handwork to insure fine tone quality. New aero bridge strengthens the sounding board and further improves the tone quality. Body of figured mahogany; top of selected spruce. All edges trimmed with black and white celluloid. Stripe inlay on back. Mahogany neck with rosewood veneer headpiece. Ebonized oval fingerboard trimmed with black and white celluloid and inlaid with pearl position ornaments. Nickel plated patent heads with white buttons, geared to 12 to 1 ratio. Hand rubbed lacquer finish. Concert size. Two instruction books, 3 picks, a steel bar and adjustable nut for playing Hawaiian style included. Postpaid.
12T217¼
$14.65

The Student

Many ask as much as $8.00 for no better quality. Standard size. Body of hardwood. Natural finish top, edge and soundhole inlaid with colored wood block marquetry and bound with black celluloid. Back and sides finished in deep walnut stain. Brass gear patent heads. Instruction book and pick included. Postpaid.
12T204¼
$4.98
12T205¼
Same as above, but in ¾ or women's size. Postpaid.
$4.98

Postpaid
$4.98
12T204¼

12T4432 Steel Bar, adjustable nut, two picks and instruction book for playing above guitars in Hawaiian style. Postpaid. 40c

The Flash

A leader in an inexpensive guitar. Deep shaded brown finish. Made of hardwood throughout. Heavy ebonized fingerboard accurately fretted, and with 3 position dots. Steel plate brass gear patent heads; ebonized bridge and nickel plated tailpiece. Instruction book and pick included. We Pay the Postage.
12T202¼
$3.85

$3.85 Postpaid

The Pearlette

Here's an unusually beautiful and sweet toned guitar. Entire body of fine mahogany with pearlette fingerboard, headpiece and guardplate. Top edge and sound hole are beautifully trimmed with wood block inlay in a pleasing combination of red, blue, green and mahogany. All edges are trimmed with white celluloid binding. The sparkling sheen of the pearlette sets off the rich dark brown finish. Nickel plated patent heads geared to 12 to 1 ratio with white buttons. Standard size. Two instruction books, three picks, a steel bar and adjustable nut for Hawaiian style of playing included. A Big Value. Postpaid.
12T214¼
$12.75
Tenor Guitar
12T215¼
Same as above, but 4 string tenor guitar (played like a tenor banjo). Also can be played like Ukulele. Instruction book and pick included.
$11.65

We Pay the Postage

inest **SUPERTONE** Professional Guitars
$400 *on Easy Monthly Payments* $550
Easy Payment   Easy Payment

GUITARS AND GEAR

H.C. Speir ran a music store in Jackson, Mississippi, during the 1920s and '30s and arranged recording sessions for Charley Patton, Skip James, Son House,

What kinds of guitars did the early bluesmen play?

and Robert Johnson, to name a few. He told collector/researcher Gayle Wardlow that his customers preferred the Stella guitars that sold for $9.95. Speir's recollection was borne out by House and fellow Mississippian Bukka White; both said they started on Stella instruments, which were manufactured by the Oscar Schmidt Co. in New Jersey and distributed in the South by St. Louis Music. Also popular were Washburn guitars, made by Chicago's Lyon and Healy and handled by mail-order giant Montgomery Ward. Lemon Jefferson cradles a Lyon and Healy instrument in his only known photo. Sears and Roebuck's famous catalog, the "wish book" where many rural pickers got their first guitars, also included a line of inexpensive guitars built by Harmony and other Chicago firms.

The popularity of these instruments had more to do with their availability and low price than playability or superior sound. Many models had tailpieces instead of the fixed pin bridges common on more expensive flattops; and virtually all of them had transverse, or ladder, top bracing instead of the Martin-style X pattern. Three or four of these bulky braces ran from side to side above and below the sound-hole, often accompanied by a substantial bridge patch. Though the purpose of this design was to cut manufacturing costs, these old guitars have a distinctive, twangy sound, and many of them are quite loud.

It's not that the blues players felt any attachment to these instruments, however; the few who ever made any money invariably ditched their Stellas in favor of pricier items. Speir recalled, for example, that when Memphis Minnie and Kansas Joe returned to the Delta in 1930 after the success of her salacious "Bumble Bee" recording, the principal trapping of their newfound notoriety was a pair of gleaming Nationals.

What guitar is best for playing slide?

Back when *vintage* referred to wine, *good for slide* was a tacit dismissal of beaters that were nearly useless for anything else (i.e., a plywood Harmony with storage space between the strings and fingerboard). Now that slide guitar and budget Harmony guitars hold a somewhat more elevated position in the acoustic firmament, the description still has some merit.

A guitar with a bright sound—biased toward the mids and high end—and higher-than-average action is a logical choice for the slide player. Intonation is not as big an issue when you're seldom fretting in the higher positions, and stout action makes for cleaner bottle-necking. Some of the cheapo boxes of yore fill the slide bill admirably.

That doesn't mean that guitars of pedigree are unsuitable. On his milestone 1941 Library of Congress debut, Muddy Waters played producer Alan Lomax's Martin. Bukka White, whose Stella gave up the ghost during his 1940 OKeh recording date, crafted slide masterpieces like "Jitterbug Swing" and "Streamline Special" on a Gibson borrowed from Big Bill Broonzy. Starting with bottleneck boss Tampa Red, and up to the present, the weapon of choice for many players (including this writer) has been the National resonator guitar. The superior volume and high-register sustain of these instruments make it easier to get the decisive attack and smooth legato that distinguishes slide guitar music.

No matter what ax you choose, an essential feature of a guitar that's good for slide is its setup. *Heavier* and *higher* describe the ideal strings and action. Most acoustic guitars (except some lightly built small-body models) will accept medium-gauge strings, and a common device is to use a medium (.013–.056) set, subbing heavier wire (say, .015 and .018) for the unwound first and second strings. I prefer an even heavier set for my Nationals: a custom-made, round-core .016–.060 set. If you are unsure whether your guitar can handle heavier strings, check with a good repairer before you put them on.

At least as important as strings is action. I've found that I can set my guitars up so that the bottom side of the first string passes a full 3/32 of an inch from the crown of the 12th fret without compromising the intonation or making the guitar too hard to fret up the neck. Use these suggestions as a rule of thumb. Experiment with strings and setup until you find a good balance between tone and playability.

No. There was a time when vintage guitars were better than new ones for playing *anything;* but the much-touted "second golden age" of guitar design is as much a reality for the rootsy twangster as it is for

Are vintage guitars better than new ones for playing blues?

other players. My contemporary Collings C-10 is equal, if not superior to, the prewar Gibsons that inspired its shape, and my 1998 National E-N is actually louder and fuller-sounding than most of the vintage brass-body, single-resonator guitars to which I've compared it. The increased quality and diversity of modern acoustics, combined with the sometimes stratospheric prices of high-end vintage instruments in good condition, makes a new guitar an important consideration for anyone in the market for an instrument they're actually going to play.

That said, vintage instruments can still be obtained (even by those of us who don't own software companies), and finding them can be fun if you know what to look for. My friend Dave Moore responded to an ad for a $100 "debro" in an Iowa City swap sheet and wound up with a 1930 National Triolian. Cases like this are increasingly rare, but they still happen. I recently got a 1932 Style 1 tricone at an affordable price by purchasing it in compromised condition (it was coming apart at the seams) and sending it to the National factory to be restored. It's by no means in mint condition, but it plays and sounds, well, like a vintage German silver tricone. I've gotten a lot of use out of it on studio slide sessions.

The blues buff on a budget can even find older instruments with that great cheap-suit look and sound in a (gasp!) vintage guitar shop. This is done by side-stepping the prominently displayed collectors' items whose prices are commensurate with the down-payment on a house and perusing the "hall of shame" racks in the back. There you may find guitars with an obvious history by Regal, Harmony, Kay, Stella, or Kalamazoo. If something looks good, check the action and examine the instrument for obvious defects, badly executed repairs, or signs of past trauma. Remember that a neck reset or fret replacement can cost hundreds of dollars. A new nut, replacement tuners, or a bridge reglue are not so expensive.

Don't pass over archtop instruments; they're some of the best values on the vintage market. And don't be put off by a few "hillbilly tracks"—signs of honest wear. Sometimes when you give a dirty old guitar a good polishing you can almost hear it say thank you.

I've gotten some wonderful guitars for a few hundred bucks or less by following these simple directives. They're the kind of guitars that make people ask, "Hey, what's that?"

New and vintage guitars along with a guitar-banjo and mandolin stand side by side in the author's collection.

Are there different types of resonator guitars? What's the difference between a National and a Dobro?

In a basic way, all resonator guitars are the same. The sound is produced when string vibrations are transmitted through the bridge into an aluminum speaker cone (or cones) mounted inside the body. Hence the generic designations: ampliphonic, resophonic, resonator guitar. They're among the most fascinating of acoustic instruments because they differ from other stringed instruments in so many ways. The bodies can be made of metal, wood, or even plastic. The necks may have a square profile for Hawaiian-style playing, or they may be conventionally rounded. The name on the headstock may be National, Dobro, Regal, Supro, Airline, Magnatone, Sho-Bro . . . the list goes on. A Brazilian variant has even been made since the '30s by the Del Vecchio Co. Depending on the model and condition, the resophonic guitar can sound like a celestial chorus or a garbage can full of newspapers falling down a fire escape. Since they first appeared in 1927, they've been a central voice in Hawaiian music, country and bluegrass, jazz, and especially the blues.

The original National instruments were designed by luthier/inventor John Dopyera at the behest of guitarist George Beauchamp. They

Bob Brozman, one of the contemporary masters of the resonator guitar, with a metal-bodied guitar, mandolin, and ukulele.

had three small resonators connected by a T-shaped aluminum bar on which the bridge was mounted. The success of this design inspired Dopyera and Beauchamp to form the National String Instrument Co. In 1928, National introduced another model (also with a metal body). It had a single nine-and-a-half inch resonator with the bridge mounted on a wooden disc attached to the small end of the cone. By 1929, John Dopyera had left National, designed a new style of resonator guitar, and (with his brothers) formed a new company, the Dobro Corp.

Like National, Dobro made standard and Hawaiian-style guitars (and a variety of other instruments). Less costly wooden bodies would largely take the place of the metals common to early Nationals, but the main difference was in the design of the resonator. Mounted in a wooden well, the Dobro resonator had a single compound cone, like a flattened W in cross-section, that opened toward the front coverplate of the guitar. The bridge was mounted on an eight-legged aluminum frame or *spider*, whose feet rested on the outer edge of the resonator. The resulting sound, sort of like a banjo played through a sustain pedal and a reverb unit, is distinct from that of National guitars, which generally have a punchier, more hornlike tone.

The National and Dobro companies eventually merged, continuing to manufacture resonator guitars and also pioneering early electric guitar technology. Ironically, the latter development helped to render National guitars obsolete, as Hawaiian, jazz, and blues players abandoned them in favor of electric instruments. Very few metal-bodied cone resonator guitars were produced after World War II. In country music, the sound of the Dobro's spider resonator persisted. This was largely due to popular records by acoustic country icon Roy Acuff and bluegrass masters Flatt and Scruggs, whose bands incorporated the Dobro played in a modified Hawaiian style.

Dobro guitars have remained in production, under various brand names, up to the present. Today, the Dobro trademark is owned by Gibson and appears on instruments with both wood and metal bodies and spider- and cone-type resonators. The manufacture of National brand guitars, single and tricone, was resumed in 1988 and, to make matters even more complicated, the company has recently introduced a square-neck, wood-body, spider-resonator guitar (Style D) to its line. In addition, instruments and resonators modeled after National and Dobro designs (and of widely varying quality) are presently made by factories and individual custom builders throughout the world as a revival of interest in the resonator guitar continues to spread.

How can I amplify my acoustic and resonator guitars?

It's ironic that one of the questions most frequently asked by acoustic musicians is, "How can I get a wire on this thing?" It's a good point to consider, especially for the live performer. After all, how often have you heard this? "Hello, I'll be your sound engineer tonight. I got here early because I wanted to be sure we had enough time to get optimum mic placement and suitable levels in the room and over the monitors. The acoustics here are great, and during the show you'll be able to hear a pin drop. By the way, that's a great shirt!" Happens all the time, right? Just the same, I always feel a little better knowing that I can augment the ambient microphone sound with a little direct input.

The oldest method of amplifying an acoustic guitar is to attach a magnetic pickup to the face under the strings. In other words, you make it into an electric guitar. Blues players from Lightnin' Hopkins to Elmore James did this by clipping a single-coil pickup from the now-defunct DeArmond company into the soundhole. It's a great sound; the DeArmond is just dirty enough, and there's not much feedback. Pre-owned DeArmonds can still be found, and there are a number of good add-on magnetic pickups currently available from companies like Seymour Duncan, Fishman, and Sunrise. Their double-coil humbucking units are cleaner and quieter than a DeArmond. Of course, clipping a five-ounce metal object to your soundhole diminishes your guitar's acoustic response, to say the least.

The alternative to a magnetic pickup—one whose electronic field picks up the vibrations of the metal strings—is a piezo transducer. These are mounted or stuck to the inside of the guitar face or under the bridge saddle and are sensitive to the vibrations of the guitar itself. They are small, and the signal is more "acoustic-sounding." Their active circuitry requires a battery or other power source, and most sound better with an outboard EQ. Notable among these, especially for resonator guitars, are Highlanders, stock equipment on many contemporary Nationals. They're loud and realistic-sounding with little or no EQ. In combination with an ambient cardioid mic to deliver all those nice crunchy metallic noises a National makes, they produce a great reso sound, even on a festival stage.

Some guitarists use a combination of magnetic pickups, piezo transducers, and even internally mounted microphones, mixing them, running an outboard EQ, and adding digital effects like reverb, delay, and compression. Experiment with this kind of setup if you've got the inclination (and money). Before I go to that kind of trouble, I'll just get out my Telecaster guitar and Vibrolux amp.

A lot of acoustic blues players have used 12-string guitars. What kind works best for blues?

From Georgia bluesmen Willie McTell and Robert (Barbecue Bob) Hicks to Louisiana folk/blues phenomenon Huddie Ledbetter and one-man-band Jesse Fuller, the 12-string guitar has been part of the acoustic blues sound since before the recording era. Once again, the instruments of choice were made by Stella. Leadbelly didn't recall the exact year he obtained his first instrument. He did remember picking cotton for a week to raise the $12 price of a guitar he'd seen in a Dallas store—one he had to have after hearing a similar model played by a medicine-show performer—that was already an integral part of his sound when he started his first stretch in prison in 1918. (Stella guitars, made by Oscar Schmidt, first appeared in 1911. The name was acquired by Harmony in 1939; and that company continued to manufacture 12-string guitars through the 1960s.)

Again, the preference for Stella 12-strings was largely based on their low price and availability. However, with its large body size, ladder bracing, and long (26½-inch) scale length, the Stella had another characteristic important to the acoustic blues player—superior volume. The instruments were, and are, often tuned well below standard pitches. Leadbelly usually tuned down four half steps (from low to high, C F B♭ E G C); McTell sometimes even lower. With the heavy, wound third, fourth, fifth, and sixth string pairs tuned in octaves, the guitars produce a resonant, booming, almost piano-like sound, one quite unlike the bright jangle of conventionally tuned instruments.

Many contemporary players also favor long-scale, ladder-braced guitars. Bluesman and 12-string adept Paul Geremia uses an instrument made in the

Paul Geremia plays a Tonk Bros. 12-string from the 1920s.

'20s by Chicago's Tonk Bros. In addition, he's recently grafted a custom neck onto the body of an old Stella six-string. Alvin Youngblood Hart plays vintage Stellas that he and his wife, Heidi, have nursed back from the compromised condition that characterizes most instruments of this type encountered today. Meanwhile, contemporary builders such as Californian Marc Silber and Yorkshireman Ralph Bown continue to champion the Stella look and sound with their guitars—including Bown's uncanny reproductions of the instruments played by Leadbelly and Barbecue Bob.

This is not to say that you have to have one of these brawny boxes tuned in the basement to get a good blues sound. Lonnie Johnson played a unique, custom-made Mexican guitar with a six-pin bridge that can be heard on his solo sides and on stomping duets with jazz pioneer Eddie Lang. Twelve-strings by Gibson, Guild, and Martin didn't appear until the 1960s. Among these, some of the Gibson B-25 and the larger B-45 models offered the bridge-and-tailpiece design that lends itself to heavier strings and lower tunings. Note that many pin-bridge guitars are unsuitable for this kind of setup.

What is a nine-string guitar, and where do I get one?

Among the unique guitars that have come out of the acoustic blues gearbox are the nine-string instruments played by Big Joe Williams, who converted them himself from six-string guitars. Nine-string guitars, with the highest three courses doubled, have been offered by manufacturers—notably Alvarez—but Big Joe's were a breed apart in both sound and appearance.

The one he's most often pictured with was cobbled out of a Harmony Sovereign. The additional strings are accommodated by a set of three-on-a plate tuners, one of which passes through a hole drilled in the end of the headstock, while the other two just sort of stick out on either side of the crown. Three strings pass over the conventional pin bridge of the guitar and attach to a trapeze tailpiece screwed to the endblock. Additional grooves in the nut and saddle complete the conversion. The feature that sets the Williams-style nine-string apart is the way in which the courses are arranged. As on a 12-string, the first two are doubled and tuned in unison. The additional

double course is the fourth (not the third), tuned in an octave. Sounds strange, but try it for blues finger-style in the key of E or slide guitar in open-G tuning, and you'll get an immediate insight into Big Joe's sound . . . rude, baby!

I was inspired to make my nine-string conversion after finding, in a bar where I was playing, a ladder-braced, jumbo Kay/Silvertone hanging as a wall decoration by a hole drilled through the headstock. Exhuming the appropriate tuners and tailpiece, along with an old DeArmond pickup, from my "box o' many things," I set about making the change, electing to drill two extra holes in the head to stabilize the additional tuners. A while later I used the instrument to play a memorial benefit for Big Joe. At this event, I

Big Joe Williams played guitars that he converted to nine-strings by doubling three of the strings.

shared the bill with Charlie Musselwhite, whose matchless feel for harmonica and guitar blues was developed in no small part during his early journey work with Williams. Backstage, Musselwhite expressed an interest in my guitar. I passed it over with a mumbled apology for its rather stiff action. He hit a Big Joe lick, smiled, and said, "Don't worry. His was even worse!"

I keep hearing about blues players who started on homemade instruments. Can you really make a guitar out of a cigar box? What is a diddley bow?

Once I was employed as "folksinger-in-residence" at a museum. Part of my presentation involved playing "archaic" American instruments, most of which I was obliged to make myself—Appalachian dulcimers, gourd fiddles and banjos . . . you name it. The instrument that elicited the greatest interest from visitors was a little four-string guitar I'd made by attaching a hand-carved neck to a wooden cigar box.

Sure, the school kids loved it—especially when I quoted rock hits like "Smoke on the Water"—but the most significant response was from the older set. In retrospect, I wish I'd recorded some of the memories of folks who recalled the whuppin' they got for dissembling a broom or screen door to obtain wire to string their first cigar-box guitar; or the fishing line they stretched over hand-carved pegs trying to get a sound even remotely guitarlike.

Russell Hibbard's well-crafted diddley bow has a unique soundhole.

The instruments I constructed were a little more sophisticated; they had frets, conventional tuners, and real strings. Also incorporated were interior end and heel blocks, balsa wood seam lining, an ice-cream-stick bridge patch, and a length of wooden dowel running end to end inside the box to keep it from collapsing. An instrument built 20 years ago using this design is still playable at this writing. Given the renewed popularity of imported cigars, wooden display boxes are now fairly easy to find; but functional stringed instruments can also be made from cookie tins, ham cans, and lard buckets.

The simplest of homemade stringed instruments is the diddley bow. The name is a slang descriptive for members of a family of instruments whose common trait is that they have only one string. People have been playing monochords since prehistoric times. Variants are still part of the folk music of West Africa, Brazil, and the American South, where the diddley bow or jitterbug, in days past, was almost invariably the first instrument of the aspiring slide guitarist.

In his epic *Land Where the Blues Began*, Alan Lomax includes a description of Delta patriarch Napoleon Strickland building such an instrument from wooden lathing, broom wire, metal brads, and glass snuff bottles in as much time as it takes him to verbally explain the process. Then, nailing the instrument across a doorway, he commences a spontaneous slide solo using the adjoining room as a sound chamber!

There are numerous examples of more guitarlike instruments with resonating bodies, machine tuners, and even electric pickups. The basic style of playing, however, remains pretty much the same regardless of the shape or size of the instrument . . . primal slide!

What are guitar-banjos, and how are they used in acoustic blues music?

Banjos with six strings and guitar-style necks were offered by makers such as S.S. Stewart as early as the 1870s. Steel strings were in common use by the turn of the 20th century, instruments with improved tone rings and wooden resonators soon thereafter. Although "guit-jos" were not as popular as their four- and five-string relations, there are a number of instances where they were used in early jazz and blues.

This contemporary six-string guitar-banjo is made by the Deering Banjo Co.

One of the first among the ranks of recording, self-accompanied bluesmen was Papa Charlie Jackson, whose studio career began in 1924. Jackson, an excellent instrumentalist, recorded over 50 titles, including the original "Salty Dog Blues," using a guitar-banjo. Guitarist Cal Smith, who played with various incarnations of the famous Louisville Jug Stompers, often doubled on guitar-banjo. So did country guitar original Sam McGee, who used one to record, among other titles, country blues like "Chevrolet Car." When Louis Armstrong's aptly named Hot Five locked horns on low-down, New Orleans–style workouts such as "Gutbucket Blues" and "Georgia Grind," the bassless and drumless ensemble was literally driven by the guitar-banjo of the incomparable Johnny St. Cyr.

Danny Barker, originally a St. Cyr protégé—and later quite a name in the jazz world himself—continued to champion what he dubbed the guit-jo throughout his long career. Barker gave me the following setup tips, which bring some extra punch and volume out of what are generally loud, punchy instruments to begin with: First, glue a piece of bone to the crown of the wooden banjo bridge ("something hard, but not so hard that you burn your strings"). Second, using a light-gauge string set, tune the instrument three half steps above standard (to G C F A♯ D G), so that when you play a C chord shape, you're actually in E♭.

Standard bearers like Barker notwithstanding, the guitar-banjo—and banjos in general—became less and less common in jazz, blues, and related styles as the jazz age evolved into the swing era. In an ironic cultural dichotomy, the single American instrument with the most easily traceable African roots was eschewed by African-American musicians, who considered it anachronous and stereotypical.

A recent revival of interest in the guit-jo, evidenced by the introduction of new models by contemporary makers and its reappearance in a variety of acoustic music formats, is a positive chapter in the recently sparse history of this musical hybrid. As Danny Barker once said, thumbing a chord on his old Vega, "There's nothing wrong with this instrument!"

A slide is a smooth, hard, tubular object that fits over a finger—most commonly the fourth, or pinky—of your fretting hand. By touching, rather than pressing down on, a string or group of strings with the slide

What are the basic types of slides, and how do I find one that's right for me?

and moving it up and down the fingerboard, it's not hard to create a *glissando,* or slurred effect, and to play intervals smaller than the half steps delineated by the frets. Meanwhile, the other fingers are free to stop notes and chords in the usual way. It's a guitar technique that has been used in blues music since well before the recording era, and it's still in common use—and being expanded—today.

There are two general categories of slides: found and made. The former includes small glass pill bottles, bone sections from beef or ham shanks, and metal objects such as socket wrenches. (An archaic slide style involves holding the handle of a knife between two fingers and playing with its metal spine.) Made slides can be cut from pieces of metal tubing or from the neck of a glass bottle, which is why the style is often referred to as *bottleneck guitar.* Metal pipe, such as copper or brass plumbing conduit, can be cut into suitable lengths with a

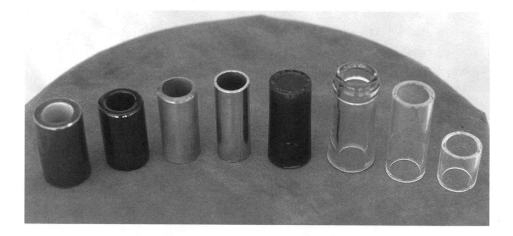

You can choose from slides of many shapes, sizes, and materials.

hacksaw—the rough ends smoothed with a fine mill file and sandpaper. One of my favorite slides was made for me by a gunsmith out of a case-hardened 12-gauge shotgun barrel.

Glass bottle necks are harder to cut by hand, but if scored to a sufficient depth with a three-cornered file or a garnet saw, they can be snapped off without serious mishap. (If you really feel you need to try this, protect your hands and eyes.) Once again, smooth off any sharp edges. Big Joe Williams has described the even chancier method of wrapping a length of string soaked in coal oil around the bottleneck, burning it off, and breaking the glass at the resultant heat fracture. I actually got this to work . . . once.

These days, the easiest way to obtain a slide is to buy one. Glass, metal, and ceramic items of every description can be had in any music store that orders from the Bruno catalog, from the hefty, flared brass slides made by Latch Lake to the light Pyrex tubes from Dunlop. I still prefer a heavy glass bottle neck and, by good fortune, I was able to find a slide guitarist and craftsman who'd make them to my specs. Several years ago, I was playing in Tucson, Arizona, when Gerry Glombecki offered me one of his Original Delta Sliders (made from "100 percent recycled bottles"!). The model he showed me was a little too long, and the raised lip on one end got in my way, so he made me a few that were cut, beveled, and polished at both ends, and sized just a little shorter than my pinky finger. Soon I was carrying an assortment to shows and guitar clinics as part of my merchandise display.

Slide players were then able to compare the feel of a 44-gram, light blue Pinot Grigio to that of heavier, darker slides made from Montepulciano d'Abruzzo and aged Porfidio Tequila . . . Whoa!

No matter what your slide is made of, it should fit loosely enough so you can crook your finger slightly inside it to keep it from slipping—you'll get better vibrato and pitch control that way. Remember also that most glass bottle necks have a seam that can rasp against your strings, so rotate your slide accordingly.

Are there advantages to using fingerpicks? How do you keep them from falling off while you're playing?

Well, you can certainly play a lot louder with fingerpicks than without 'em and, unless you're one of those keratin-empowered people, they'll last a lot longer than your nails on steel strings. You either like the sound they produce or you don't; and yes, they can be awkward. It was only under duress that I started using them myself.

Back in my salad days, I was a nonpick partisan. If it was good enough for John Hurt, by God . . . you get the idea. One pickless night, I was loading out some gear after a show when a speaker cabinet fell on my right hand; the metal rim around the grill cloth severed the extensor tendon in my thumb. Weeks later, when the cast came off, I was relieved to find that reconstructive surgery had repaired the tendon. I would eventually be able to play fingerstyle guitar again.

Eventually, however, wasn't gonna cut it. I'd been out of work for nearly two months, and I needed to resume plank-spankin' forthwith. My hand was so atrophied that at first I could hardly touch my thumb to my index finger. Any nail or callus I might have had was history. I squeezed on one of those old clear plastic Dobro thumbpicks and a pair of equally worn National metal fingerpicks, taped them in place, and went back to playing happy hours. (I wasn't laughing.) I don't recommend this method for developing the technique.

Should you want to experiment with picks, start by using a set that fits snugly. At present there is no shortage of types and sizes, both metal and plastic, from which to choose. Practice familiar fingerstyle themes at first. Get used to the fact that you don't have to dig in as hard as you would with bare fingers. If you're accustomed to playing down-strums with your fingers, well, you'll just have to stop! When using picks in the conventional manner, your thumb plays downstrokes, your fingers upstrokes. If you think that's limiting, listen to Reverend Gary Davis and Merle Travis, and get back to me later. Check out the gear and styles of guitarists whose playing you enjoy. As with slide guitar, everybody has a little different way of doing things.

I still use a plastic thumbpick (Golden Gate No. 2) and metal fingerpicks (ProPik No. 2 standard, no tape) for live performances and in most studio situations. They're especially handy for getting the full dynamic range out of a resonator guitar. I also like to maintain enough fingernail and callus that I can play without 'em if I want to.

What kind of strings do you use? This is not so much a question as it is a standard greeting among guitarists, expressing a commonality that transcends musical style. We all use strings! There's even a bit of humorous folklore that has Saint Peter asking this question of a picker seeking passage through the pearly gates.

In the material world, a guitarist selects strings that are appropriate for his or her guitar and playing style. Remember that string gauges shouldn't have a lot to do with your guitar's playability. If you're having a hard time pressing the strings against the frets, either your guitar is out of adjustment or you need to practice more. The main characteristic of various string types and gauges is the way they make your instrument sound.

Virtually all blues players use steel-core strings. The ascendancy of the guitar as a blues voice is concurrent with their introduction. You can't play slide guitar on nylon strings. Today, as with all gear and accessories, there are many kinds of strings from which you can assemble your ideal set.

Most acoustic guitarists use bronze-wound strings; but some—especially adherents of the resonator guitar—prefer those wound with nickel-steel alloy. The latter are also more compatible with magnetic pickups. The standard acoustic string set includes a wound third string. Some blues guitarists, John Hammond, for example, substitute a heavy (.024) plain string. There's a difference in sound, and they're also less likely to break.

My one preference is for strings with a round steel core, rather than the hexagonal wire presently in common use. There's a noticeable difference in sound, and the hand-wound sets I order from Guadalupe Custom Strings last twice as long as conventional hex-core units. (They also cost more . . . I like that.)

As previously noted, I generally use heavier gauges—but there are exceptions. Some of my instruments, such as the small, light, slotted-headstock guitars from the early 1900s, and smaller-bodied Martins, are not made to accept heavy strings; and they actually sound better when strung with lighter gauges. This is also true of guit-jos, especially if you tune them above standard guitar pitches as described earlier.

If you have more than one or two guitars, you may want to look into obtaining a gauge kit—a box of strings arranged by gauge from light/plain to heavy/wound much like a file cabinet. Then you can spend hours you would have wasted watching network television tweaking your favorite boxes until they sound "just so."

Most early blues was played on cheap, functional guitars like these Supertones featured in the 1929 Sears, Roebuck, and Co. catalog.

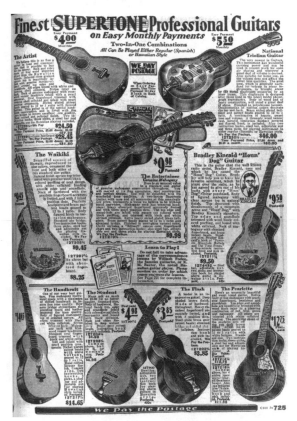

TECHNIQUES AND TUNINGS

Just playing songs is best, as far as I've been able to tell. In a workshop situation with never-before fingerpickers, I usually select something short, pretty, and melodic with an alternating bass line to start. User-friendly arrangements can be found in the music of logical players such as Mance Lipscomb, Mississippi John Hurt, Frank Stokes, or Etta Baker—songs with basic chord shapes that allow the players to concentrate on their tone, meter, and picking technique.

I like the sound of fingerpicked guitar blues, but I don't know how to start learning the style. Are there studies or exercises I can use to develop my coordination?

I start with a rendition of the song, to be sure it's one we all like, and then demonstrate the thumbpicked bass line that follows the chord changes—the heart of any fingerstyle arrangement. Then, at a slow pace, I demonstrate the melody line, which is picked with the fingers. If some of the folks start looking really sad at that point, I'll pause and interject an anecdote about something Buddha-like that Mance or Etta once did, or describe the self-destructive fantasies I entertained as a kid before, one otherwise unremarkable day, my thumb just started going back and forth over the strings all by itself. Then, it's back to *boom-chang*.

One practice habit I recommend—one I still use myself when I've heard or written something I can't play—is to thumb the bass line alone while humming the melody to yourself. After a couple of hours (just kidding!), play the fingerpicked melody while tapping your foot and singing or thinking the bass line to the beat. When it gets dark, take a candle and a live chicken and go to the . . . no, no! Forget I mentioned it.

There are a lot of good books and videos out there for the beginning fingerstylist. There are also some fine filmed sequences of great guitarists playing live—many of these are priceless. Of course, go to as many live shows as you can, and sit down front. Don't be shy about asking performers guitar-related questions, even if some of us do seem a little cranky at times.

Guitar camps and workshops offer an opportunity to learn firsthand from players with different styles and approaches to presenting the music. They are also good meeting places for people with shared musical direction who want to exchange information, share experiences, and jam.

Is there life after alternating bass?

Uhh . . . yes! When a guitarist has developed his or her reptile brain enough that alternating-bass fingerpicking no longer requires a conscious effort, that part of the cognitive mentality can be devoted to other issues (e.g., "Want mushrooms on your half?").

Once you can sustain a two-note bass line over basic chord shapes and pick a melody or riff over it, there's a substantial repertoire that can be absorbed without much difficulty. Also, it's relatively easy to devise variations, tonal and rhythmic, on an alternating-bass pattern. These include *pedal point* (where one voice changes and the other remains fixed), *counterpoint* (where high and low voices move toward or away from each other), and *walking bass/chord lines* (where the low voice ascends or descends and the upper moves with it, as in stride piano).

Guitarists often ask me if it wouldn't be easier to start with a steady, one-note bass line for each chord—they often mention Texas bluesman Lightnin' Hopkins. My experience is that it's easier to learn to play a solid beat, which is absolutely essential, in the alternating-bass style on strongly melodic material. Hopkins' relaxed, improvisational style is a good deal more complex than it sounds!

If you're asking if there's a way to still be cool without knowing how to make your thumb go back and forth, I can't help you . . . and if you want to play lead, go get a Strat. Acoustic blues has always been mainly fingerpicking territory. Even the great electric blues soloists, from Guitar Slim to Magic Sam to Alberts Collins and King, have gone pickless.

Nothing wrong with plectrums per se, though. . . . Blues was an essential theme for early country greats like Jimmie Rodgers and the Delmore Brothers—who used "straight picks," as they were called. The Delmores especially developed a great blues/boogie sound by pairing flatpicked standard and tenor guitars. Bluegrass pickers, notably stylistic touchstone Doc Watson, are fond of borrowing from the Delmores' high-octane blues repertoire.

Blues is also basic to the vocabulary of acoustic jazz guitarists from Teddy Bunn to Dick McDonough. Bluesiest of all, perhaps, were Lonnie Johnson and Eddie Lang, who moonlighted as a guitar duet between their gigs with Louis Armstrong and Paul Whiteman. Although both Johnson and Lang were adept with or without a pick, workouts like "Two-Tone Stomp" and "Bullfrog Blues" hold an exalted place in the plectral pantheon.

Hokum hotshot Ikey Robinson picked some search-and-destroy solos on his own material and in support of the diminutive, cross-dressing wailer Frankie "Half Pint" Jaxon. The same can be said for Quillian Brothers Rufus and Ben, who did some fancy cross-picking on suggestive offerings like "I'm Satisfied," and Kansas Joe was definitely totin' tortoiseshell for some of his rolling bass-chord work in support of his better half, Memphis Minnie.

If you subscribe to the opinion that a lot of the best rock 'n' roll is just country blues in overdrive, then dig rockabillies like Johnny Cash and Elvis whatshisname. They strummed the you-know-what out of their Martins on hits like "Get Rhythm" and "That's All Right, Mama." I especially like Cash's trick of threading a playing card through the strings just in front of the bridge—the poor man's snare drum.

So, I guess there's a place for picks after all. What'd I do with that thing?

**Which open and alternate
tunings are most commonly
used in blues?**

The two principal open tunings have old, vernacular
American names that I still like to use: Vastopol and
Spanish. Rather than conceptualize tunings by a letter name that corresponds to a particular key (i.e.,
"open A" or "open D"), it's useful to think of them in terms of the intervals of which they're composed. That's what these names are about.

Vastopol tuning, usually an open D or E major chord, is named for
a popular 19th-century guitar instrumental called "Sebastopol." (It's a
port on the Black Sea, the scene of a pivotal engagement in the
Crimean War!) Here are the notes of the D and E versions of Vastopol,
low to high, followed by the scale degrees for each note. The 1 refers
to the *tonic* or *root* note of the chord, 5 is the fifth, and 3 is the third.

D	A	D	F♯	A	D
E	B	E	G♯	B	E
1	5	1	3	5	1

Spanish tuning also takes its name from a parlor guitar favorite,
"Spanish Fandango." Here's the most common G version, followed by
the A version and the scale degrees:

D	G	D	G	B	D
E	A	E	A	C♯	E
5	1	5	1	3	5

Notice that in Vastopol, the first degree of the scale (or *root*), corre-
sponding to the key of the tuning, falls on the sixth, fourth, and first
strings. In Spanish it's the fifth and third strings. Observe also that
both tunings are composed of the first, third, and fifth degrees of the
major scale—comprising a major chord triad.

Open minor tunings are also used in blues music. The best example
in the acoustic genre is the music of Skip James. His "cross minor" tuning
is reached by lowering the third string in Vastopol a half step, as follows:

D	A	D	F	A	D
E	B	E	G	B	E
1	5	1	3m	5	1

I've also gotten some use out of a minor variant of Spanish tuning, which works especially well for playing slide guitar:

D	G	D	G	B♭	D
E	A	E	A	C	E
5	1	5	1	3m	5

Another tuning commonly used in acoustic blues is called dropped-D: simply lower the sixth string in standard tuning from E to D (a whole step) and play in the key of D. Examples of its use can be found in the playing of Tommy Johnson ("Canned Heat"), Willie McTell ("Statesboro Blues"), and Lonnie Johnson. Speaking of Lonnie Johnson, he sometimes used an open sixth tuning, like Spanish but with the first string raised a whole step to a major sixth.

D	G	D	G	B	E
5	1	5	1	3	6

With some practice, it's not hard to recognize these tunings by ear.

How do you learn guitar parts off records and tell what tunings and chord shapes are being used?

Sometimes you can find the information you want in the liner notes—Yazoo reissues are especially good for this. Techniques and tunings have been transcribed and demonstrated by just about every touring and recording artist in the blues/roots genre (including myself).

As you absorb new material, try to develop your ear rather than just learning by rote where to place your fingers. Some lessons along these lines from your local guitar or voice teacher won't hurt. A lot of people have the misconception that the blues is somehow basically different from other kinds of music. It's not.

For the more experienced player, it's fun to sit down with a record or tape and try to nail the parts by ear. The problem with older recordings is pitch. Recorded performances of early blues were often sped up slightly in the mastering process to make them sound a little brighter, or simply to fit them on one three-minute side of a 78-rpm disc. Furthermore, early blues guitar soloists were not always tuned to standard pitches, so you have to rely on your ear for intervals to suss out the tunings and chord shapes.

Sometimes, the artist makes it easy. At the beginning of his finger-busting "Police Dog Blues," Blind Blake politely spells out his Vastopol mode in harmonics. Muddy Waters, when asked by field recordist Alan Lomax what tuning he's in, laconically answers, "Spanish," and then deliberately strums the guitar strings. Mostly, though, you're on your own. Here are a few navigational devices.

If it's a slide guitar piece, it's in an open tuning. Which one? If the lowest bass note you hear is the tonic note of the key, it's usually Vastopol. This is also true if there's a bottleneck figure that slides up to the third and then sounds an open note on the first string. Listen to Bukka White and Blind Willie Johnson for good examples of this. If the tonic note on the high end is repeatedly played with a slide, as in Robert Johnson's "Walkin' Blues," the guitar is probably in Spanish. (Johnson is notoriously tuned sharp—to open B♭, or even B!)

In standard tuning, if the piece has a "raggy" sound, like a lot of Blake or early Broonzy, the usual suspects are the keys of C or G. The key of E can often be identified by the low open note in the bass, and the characteristic hammer-on to the major third on the third string, first fret. Likewise, in A, you'll often hear the slurred third that country bluesers like to play on the second string at the first to second fret. Vastopol and dropped-D are easily confused on nonslide pieces. In the latter, the high tonic note in the first position is obviously fretted (second string, third fret), not open.

Don't be afraid of taking a wrong turn. I was once approached after a show by a guitarist who'd figured out my version of Charlie Poole's "Milwaukee Blues" in Spanish (open G). I play the song in dropped-D capoed at the fifth fret. "You know how to hurt a guy, don'tcha?" he groaned.

Frankly, I thought his arrangement was at least as good as mine.

What is a thumb roll?

Sounds like something on a sushi menu, doesn't it?

The thumb roll is a fingerpicking technique most commonly used in conjunction with alternating-bass-style picking. In straight alternating-bass picking, the thumb plays four beats per measure. The first and third beats are usually the lower bass notes, while the second and fourth beats involve a higher bass note or chord partial. When playing a thumb roll, insert a still lower bass note that anticipates one or more of these beats, generally the "on" beats (count: a-one, two, a-three, four, etc.). Simply roll your thumb over two adjacent bass strings to get this effect. Good examples can be heard in the playing of ragtime/blues guitarist Blind Blake (for example, in the opening bars of his classic "Diddie Wah Diddie"). Demonstrations are included in my video *Blues/Roots Guitar* (Homespun Tapes) and my book *Roots and Blues Fingerstyle Guitar* (String Letter Publishing).

The gentle, rolling style of Mississippi John Hurt is a great starting point for any blues fingerstyle player.

How do you play single-note phrases when you're fingerpicking?

If the lick I want to hit is on the lower strings, I use downstrokes of my thumb. On the treble strings, I do upstrokes of my index and/or middle fingers. This works fine for quarter-note or even eighth-note phrases. If I want to get busier than that, the approach is different.

To play fast passages of 16th notes or triplets on single strings, the technique that usually works best is to address the string(s) with alternate down- and upstrokes of the thumb and index finger (with the thumb striking the "on" beats). It's possible to simulate the sound of flatpicking this way. The best example that comes to mind in blues as I write this is some of Bill Broonzy's more energetic early sides; it's also the operative mode of the Hawaiian-style soloist in overdrive.

Another way to play single-note fills is to incorporate a thumb and finger roll pattern like that used by bluegrass banjoists; instead of playing the notes in a linear manner, arpeggiate a series of chord partials that contain the notes you want. The convention-

al method of playing fast passages most used by classical and fla-
menco guitarists employs upward *rest strokes* of the fingers. This
works fine on steel-string guitar as well but, for some reason, it's
not used much.

**I'd like to learn more about
playing blues using the
Hawaiian or lap style of
guitar. Can you recommend
recordings and instructional
material?**

Back in the '20s, when the first recordings of hot guitar were made, people were going bananas for
Hawaiian-style guitar. The level of virtuosity displayed by islanders like Sol Hoopii inspired players
in a number of styles, including blues, to perfect their
technique.

William "Casey Bill" Weldon did session work
with Big Bill Broonzy and Bumble Bee Slim in addition to his 1930s
solo sides. He was an authoritative player with a "this is me" style
in Spanish tuning, and the sound of his National is immediately
recognizable. Less recorded than Weldon, but a definite "should
hear," is Oscar Woods from Shreveport. Hawaiian style lends itself
to more melodic, less riff-oriented playing than bottleneck slide,
and Woods was no exception. He could play hot or sweet, gospel to
gutbucket. Charley Patton was famous for throwing his guitar
around, and it sometimes wound up on his lap—as on his "High
Sheriff Blues."

As I've suggested before, not all great blues was played by "bluesmen," and this is especially true of Hawaiian guitar style. Among the
country kahunas, a standout is Jimmie Tarlton, but even Gene Autry
(yes, the same one!) could get pretty lowdown.

Some of the best acoustic blues to be heard in the lap style can be
found on the recordings of hula hotshots like the aforesaid Hoopii and
King Bennie Nawahi—ouch, they're good!

After the introduction of electric instruments in the '30s, acoustic
steel went away fast and, with the exception of bluegrass and country
Dobro, it stayed gone for a while. In recent years, though, there's been
a grassroots resurgence, led by squires of the square-neck like Bob
Brozman. There's no shortage of instructional material for the lap
player, from Brozman's demonstrations of his virtuosity to Kelly Joe
Phelps' presentation of his unique style. There are a lot of licks to be

learned from Dobro and electric steel players, from early western swingers to contemporary blues master Freddie Roulette, and Brozman mails to remind us that a lot of bottleneck slide licks can be adapted to the lap.

I tell you another thing . . . A good blues man don't play so much when he singing because, when you move them fingers too devilish fast, it takes away from your voice.

—Big Bill Broonzy, from an interview with Alan Lomax

All these hot licks are fine, but all I really want to do is accompany my own singing. Any tips for the blues singer/guitarist?

It's good to remember that country blues guitar style is principally a vehicle for vocal accompaniment. (Robert Johnson, hot as he was, never recorded a solo.) Even if you're just a strummer, though, you can develop a few techniques to make your guitar part correspond more closely to your vocal line.

First, it helps to pick out the melody of the song you're singing. A common device in blues is to underscore a sung phrase by doubling it with your instrument. Also, knowing where the melody notes lie on your fingerboard will help you to choose chord shapes that complement your singing.

Any chord can be played more than one way. When playing accompaniment, a guitarist often tries to pitch the melody note highest in the chord shape. This is done by using different chord *inversions,* which are simply ways of playing the same notes in a different order. At right are inversions of A7, D7, and E7 chords.

By mixing and matching these inversions, you can make the accompaniment to, say, a 12-bar blues sound a little more colorful than if you just used one inversion of each chord. Of course, when you're playing a simple accompaniment, just as when playing a hot solo, good tone and solid rhythm are most important.

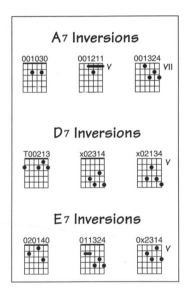

The first (lowest-pitched) A7 inversion has an E note (the fifth) on top. The second has the A (root) uppermost. In the third inversion, C♯ (third) is highest.

Why should I learn a bunch of hard songs by old guys? I just want to play my own style.

If you don't know what tradition is, how do you know what to depart from? Blues players are a remarkable set of individuals. There is no group of musicians who ascribe more importance to personal style (or less to formal training). At the same time, creative stylists in blues have always been ready to acknowledge their influences. Eric Clapton gives it up to B.B. King, who cites Lonnie Johnson and Bukka White. Bukka White learned from Frank Stokes and Charley Patton. Patton learned by following a songster named Henry Sloan—a man whose music we'll never hear, one whose name we know only because he gave guitar lessons to the "father" of the Delta blues.

Of course you want to sound

Blues is a long chain: Bukka White, shown here on stage in 1970, learned from Charley Patton and Frank Stokes, and in turn inspired B.B. King.

like yourself. What's the point in simply reciting by rote the ideas of someone else? But there's still no University of the Blues, and if you want to get some chops going and develop any degree of mastery on your instrument, you'd better do some homework along the line.

Want to know the basics of fingerstyle guitar? They can be summed up in three words: Mississippi John Hurt. I suppose it would be possible to create a great, original slide guitar style without paying some attention to the music of Tampa Red, and if that's the route you want to take, I wish you the best of luck.

I recently attended a guitar clinic where the curriculum included some music theory. Do you really have to know that stuff to play the blues?

No, but, if you don't, you'd better have an ear like a satellite dish. Students of mine who initially wince when I say the *t* word often change their tune (literally) after spending some time with my customary single-page handout on basic theory. Here's some information that will help you find the notes you want to play on your guitar's fingerboard, and to build useful chord shapes without having to consult a book every time you change keys. Let's start with a chromatic scale (see Musical Examples appendix). Adjacent notes are separated by an interval of a half step. Each half step is the equivalent of a fret on your guitar; so if your open A string is stopped at the first fret, it sounds as A♯, at the second fret as B, and so on. A diatonic scale is composed of whole and half steps (two half steps equaling one whole step). As we've already seen, a scale with blues tonality can be constructed by adding the flatted third and fifth and substituting the flatted seventh. (The flatted seventh is so commonly used that the term *seventh* usually refers to it, and the seventh degree of a diatonic major scale is referred to as a *major seventh*.)

A chord is defined as any three or more notes that sound together in harmony. The common major triad is composed of the first, third, and fifth degrees of a major scale. An A-major chord is spelled this way: A C♯ E. A major triad can be altered by adding another scalar element. The (flatted) seventh is commonly used in blues. For A major, the flatted seventh is a G, so an A7 chord includes the notes A, C♯, E, and G.

Knowing the relative values of whole- and half-step intervals that compose scales, and the larger ones that form chords, will help you learn to recognize them by ear. For example, people often ask me how I change quickly from one tuning to another on stage without having to use an electronic device. That's how.

PRACTICING AND PERFORMING

"When you were first pickin' it up, how long did you have to practice every day to learn how to play?" Alan Lomax once asked Muddy Waters.

How much do you practice, and what do you play?

"An hour and a half to two hours," Muddy replied.

"Every day?"

"Every day."

The last two words in this dialogue are most important. The saying goes: If you don't practice for one day, you know it. Two days, the band knows it. Three days, everybody knows it.

When I'm off the road and can manage regular daily practice, I take advantage of the opportunity. My practice area is arranged with a few instruments, some tab and manuscript paper, a cassette player/recorder, and a basket of picks, slides, capos, etc., within easy reach. With what a friend once called "the sleep habits of a fruit bat," I'm often up at dawn. While that first pot of coffee is brewing, I perform ablutions, make a wardrobe selection, and slip on my mood ring. By then, the joe's ready, and there's usually time for more than an hour of uninterrupted practice.

Unless I've been out of the loop for a couple of days, I don't spend a lot of time on scales or similar warm-up exercises. Practice falls generally into two categories: maintaining and developing repertoire and improving technique. Doing the former, I may single out a piece or two from my set list that haven't been sounding the way I'd like them to and run through them a few times to tighten them up. There's always a "bull-pen" selection—a new song that's not quite ready for performance—and this gets similar attention. This is also a time when new arrangement or song ideas are likely to occur to me, and I tape them or jot them down.

To improve my technique, I sometimes single out a solo or passage by a guitarist who's better than I am and obsess on it until the coffee's gone. I also devise exercises of my own to maintain and improve elements like thumb and finger rolls, good slide tone and intonation, smooth transitions between chord inversions, etc. I don't usually use a metronome, but I keep one handy. If a passage presents a consistent problem in execution, I slow it down until I can get a handle on it. I try to avoid what guitarists call "practicing your best licks"—that is, spending a lot of time playing things I already know well. Also called noodling, this habit is particularly common among blues players.

On an ideal day, I'll find time to extend my regimen to include an evening session—usually a little more relaxed. I even have a little ¾-size Kay flattop that I actually keep in bed so I can play those "fruit bat" licks that sometimes wake me up nights . . . but that, admittedly, is taking the whole thing a little further than necessary.

I have kids and a day job, so two hours a day is out of the question. Can I keep my chops up and learn new material?

No reason why not. I don't have a day gig, nor do I have to entertain a daily dialogue with children, but I do have a tour schedule, and I have to entertain a daily dialogue with club managers and events promoters (who can't be sent to their rooms). When practice time is in short supply, the "every day" rule becomes even more important. I don't know exactly why, but you can retain more by practicing 20 minutes a day than by cramming for two and a half hours once a week. Be extra aware of keeping fresh material in the mix. Select a practice piece that presents a bit of a challenge—in a new tuning, perhaps, or incorporating an unfamiliar technique—and devote part of your daily time to it until you have it pat. If you play exclusively for your own enjoyment, be sure to select music you enjoy, and don't push yourself too hard.

You can bring your instrument to work with you and practice there; I've heard of people doing so (although I've never heard of an employer saying, "We felt you deserved this raise in salary because of the way you play slide guitar every day during your coffee break"). Children, especially smaller ones, are generally curious about their parents' practice habits (or any other activity obviously unrelated to obtaining candy for them). Reward their inquiring intellects by giving them ukuleles (or cigar boxes!). The family that plays together . . .

Playing the guitar makes my hands hurt. Am I doing something wrong?

There's no right or wrong way to play acoustic or country blues, but if you have chronic pain—something more serious than the sore fingertips that result from an all-night jam session—have a care about your mitts. A stretched or damaged tendon can take as long to heal itself as a cracked bone.

To begin with, be sure your instrument is properly set up. If you're not sure about this, get a good repair person to have a look at it. The diagnosis is usually free, and improving an instrument's action by adjusting the truss rod and/or reprofiling the nut and saddle is not a costly operation. Remember that a very low action, as preferred by some rock and jazz players, will create unwanted buzzing when you dig in country blues style.

If your guitar's OK and your hands still hurt a lot, examine the way you play. Cramming, not playing for days on end, and then starting a long session without warming up can give you a cramp. Remember that although there's no cut-and-dried way to play in this style, country blues players have always been a manually economical lot. If you're figuring out a piece by ear and feel, and you find yourself making an unusually long or awkward stretch, remember the adage: If it's not comfortable, you're probably doing it wrong.

What equipment do you use on stage?

In an ideal situation, two microphones, one for guitar and one for vocal, are sufficient. On rare occasions, I

Steve James on stage, with two microphones and a DI wire.

encounter situations where no amplification at all is needed (a 12th-century church in the Wicklow Mountains of Ireland, or the vaulted functions room of an old Austrian inn). It's a mistake, however, to assume that ideal acoustics and high-quality sound equipment will be available at every show, and when they're not, no amount of knob twiddling will get the sound to the back row. For this reason, I have the guitars I use most on stage fitted with pickups whose signals can be used to augment that of the guitar mic in the main speakers—to boost weak frequencies or simply to afford more volume without feedback. The signal from a transducer can also be run, by itself, through the monitors so I can hear my instrument clearly while playing and tuning without the feedback that so often comes from an ambient mic. (Note that, unless it's absolutely impossible to hear the room sound, I usually ask the engineer to turn the monitors off or to point them toward the audience in a solo performance situation.)

Why not just use the on-board gear and dispense with the ambient mic? Simply because I like the noise that comes from the outside of my guitar—all that scraping, banging, and crunching goes with the territory. One thing I don't like is a long, obsessive, tedious sound check. They seldom make you sound any better, and the techs do imitations of you after you finally leave the stage to go sulk in your dressing room.

The one thing I like to have on stage that's most often not there has nothing directly to do with the way I sound: it's the backless, bar-type stool specified in my four-line stage rider. Why these things have become so scarce, even in bars, is something I haven't been able to figure out.

No one who spends this much time arranging their performance schedule and traveling to the shows feels much trepidation when it's finally time to get up

Do you ever get stage fright?

there and play. I understand that performers in the highest echelons of pop music engage preshow acupuncturists and hypnotists to help them summon the inner power to trod the boards. You don't see much of this at blues festivals, where the problem is usually getting the performers off the stage, not on.

I hear this question raised a lot, though. A lot of aspiring blues players have performing ambitions, and despite what the old songs say about blacksnakes and hellhounds, the creatures that torment them most are butterflies. If you've got problems along this line, there are a few things you can do about it. The first is to be sure of your material. Choose songs that tell a story you like, and practice until you're sure of your ability to present them in a relaxed manner. Know your guitar part well enough that you can smile while you're playing it.

Treat the stage as a special place, and you're more likely to feel special when you're on it. Put together a couple of stage outfits—glad rags that make you feel good when you wear 'em. It doesn't have to be a tux or a spandex jumpsuit (and puh-leez don't dress like the Blues Brothers!), but . . . sweatpants!? Really. Think of the audience as your friends, and they'll be more likely to act that way. One way to develop this attitude is to start by playing for and with your friends.

Whether it's an acoustic or resonator guitar, a solo or ensemble performance, I use two microphones. One is placed near the neck/body junction; the other over

How do you mic and record your guitars in the studio?

the body itself—usually near the bridge. I don't like to place the mic directly over the soundhole for two reasons. One is that it's liable to pick up undesirable "wolf tones." Another is that I'm liable to hit it with my picking hand, especially when I'm tapping or slapping on the upper part of the fingerboard. On a resonator guitar, I've found that a good place for the body mic is on the treble side of the cover plate. I don't have strict mic preferences, but I've gotten a lot use out of the 414 model made by AKG, and most studios seem to have some around. I've never heard anyone say, "I'm not playing another note until you

get that Neumann out of my sight!" and, on my recent *Boom Chang* project we got some nice guitar sounds using Milab mics. In addition to recording everything as hot as possible (aka "red-lining it"), I'm sold on the idea of throwing up a mic or two in the room and using that signal to add depth to the sound, instead of adding a lot of digital reverb.

On my own projects, I've worn the producer's hat, which means, among other things, selecting a good engineer and listening carefully to his suggestions. This helps to avoid obvious pitfalls like mic phase cancellation and generally makes the tape roll faster. Speaking of tape, I still like to record with analog equipment and achieve inner peace in the glow of a vacuum tube. I used to wonder whether the latter preference was more retro posture than musicality. Recently, I remastered some of my old stuff for a compilation CD, and the engineer suggested we run the signal through an old Manley tube compressor—not for compression, just for the tube. There was an audible difference in depth and presence, especially for solo guitar!

How do you get a live sound and still wind up with mixable tracks?

If you want a live sound, the best way to get it is to record live. About 90 percent of my favorite records were made that way, and I never use overdubbing on my own albums, which have been recorded almost entirely with acoustic instruments. One reason is that I like the more spontaneous sound of a "head up" performance; and the musicians I work with are generally capable of turning in tracks devoid of "flams" in a couple of takes. The other reason is that the production budgets

I've gotten from the indie labels for whom I've recorded have precluded the possibility of spending extra time in the studio overdubbing additional parts or fixing tracks that weren't played properly to begin with.

To date, even when recording with resonator guitars, banjos, and tuba—all notorious sources of "bleed"—we haven't had to put anybody in a closet. Generally, the ensemble will be seated in a circle that allows unobstructed sight lines, and each instrument will be close-miked with a cardioid setup. Ambient mics are important in a situation like this—they often supply a road map for the subsequent mix and can diminish or obviate the need for using effects while mixing. Why use a digital effect called "large room" when you can just record in one?

Careful setup will yield enough separation so that solos can be "ridden" a little, the low end can be tightened up, and instruments and vocals can be placed where you want them in the mix. Once again, a good engineer is essential—one who smiles when he sees a bunch of people with tubas, tenor banjos, and tattoos, and ambles over to the microphone cabinet.

I don't have any professional aspirations, but some roots-minded friends and I would like to organize informal jam sessions. Ever do that kind of thing?

Certainly. Professional activities have not diminished my appreciation of music as a social vehicle. I have a number of friends here in Texas who enjoy getting together, setting out a bunch of instruments and a circle of chairs in the back room, stocking the fridge with libations, putting a pot of something on the stove, and letting it rip.

Everybody participates in a different way. One old friend of mine, an illustrator and commercial artist by trade, has considerable instrumental skills and, although he never performs in public, he often leads the pack at a jam session. His wife, a teacher who can't play an instrument and doesn't even like to sing solo, has assembled a huge loose leaf songbook, from jug band to Jimmie Rodgers, with typewritten lyrics and changes, so that the inevitable question "What do we play next?" seldom goes unanswered for long. I enjoy demoting myself to amateur status again and taking up instruments I don't usually play on stage. Sometimes after a song, the group dissolves in laughter at the shouted observation, "God! That was awful." Other times the music sounds good enough that somebody turns on a strategically placed cassette recorder. These things often go on until the wee hours. If you feel like hosting one, here are some suggestions.

Set up the music room to allow easy access and egress with chairs arranged so that several people can hear and see each other (also a table for accessories, beverages, etc.).

Set instruments on stands or wall hangers so they can be easily reached but won't be jostled as people move around. If you have a number of instruments at hand, tune them up at the beginning of the session, using an electronic device if you have one. Designate the appropriate instruments for slide and open tunings and adjust them accordingly. Just as on a gig, if everyone starts out in tune, they're more likely to stay that way. Keep some good recorded music around that can be enjoyed or discussed during breaks, as brief as those may be.

I just moved to a new town. How can I meet other people in my area who like to play this kind of music?

Go to the open-mic jam session hosted by your local blues society. Soon a 14-year-old boy will arrive (usually accompanied by his mother or father) and unpack a Stratocaster. When the kid starts playing "Little Wing," walk out the back door of the joint. Your friends will be out there, smoking cigarettes.

Seriously, your area blues and folk organizations offer great networking opportunities and often sponsor volunteer-staffed school or public programs. Visit the guitar shops around your new home . . . maybe wear a T-shirt with the National logo or a likeness of Lemon on it. Buy a couple of sets of strings and, if business is not too heavy, strike up a chat with the owner, guitar tech, or salesperson. They are likely to know your fellow travelers. If a touring act comes through town, make a point of attending the show. The level of musicality and showmanship in the contemporary acoustic blues/roots genre is presently quite high, so you'll probably enjoy what you hear and see. I've also noticed a strong spirit of commonality among people who like acoustic blues music. It's garnered friends for me all over the world.

The first thing you want to do is to be sure it's legal. In some places it's not, and you can be fined or even jailed for playing on the street ("causing a public disturbance"). In my hometown of Austin, Texas—which bills itself as the Live Music Capitol of the World you'll want to obtain a permit through the city clerk's office before you hit the bricks.

I'd like to try playing in public for tips, like the old blues musicians used to do. Anything I should know before I hit the street?

Even if you're street legal, there are certain things you don't want to do. Don't obstruct vehicular or pedestrian traffic; this can include drawing a crowd large enough to block the sidewalk or spill out into the street. Be sure you're not blocking the entrance to a public building or a private business or residence. Soliciting money is another matter. Setting out a bucket or case with a sign that reads simply "Thank you," or even something more cheerful like "Heaven Loves a Cheerful Giver," is OK. Yelling out, "Hey, fatso . . . you in the sweatpants! Dontcha like the blues?" is definitely not OK. If you're going to sell something, like a cassette or CD, make sure your permit covers vending. Be aware that many communities have noise ordinances, specific to the decibel. If you're performing without amplification, this shouldn't be a problem; but if someone makes a complaint, no matter how loud (or not) you are, you may be asked to stop.

There are recorded instances of performers who donned dark glasses to simulate the appearance of a blind street singer. This is not only illegal; it's in bad taste. Speaking of taste vs. legali-

Private study time at blues camp.

ty; it's not against the letter of the law to sing "Dirty Mother for Ya" outside a place of worship, or "Good Morning Little Schoolgirl" near a playground, but if you wind up in the slam, don't call me.

I've seen and heard street singers all over the world, and acoustic blues is a favorite medium. Some make a marginal or even comfortable living doing so. One of these is Gypsy Dave Williams, who plays the streets of York, England. I still have the green jacket he gave me one night when the British summer had turned unexpectedly cold. It had a 99-pence flea market price tag stapled to the collar, but it's keeping me warm and dry yet. I wish him, and you, the same.

RESOURCES

The following list includes one or two essential   **Recordings**
recordings by 62 of the artists mentioned in this
book. In the cases of eclectic artists (Dave Van Ronk, for example), I
chose a recent CD that typifies their acoustic blues repertoire. Many
great blues guitarists, from Lightnin' Hopkins to Muddy Waters,
played mostly electric guitar; this discography singles out some of
their acoustic work. There are presently dozens of albums by artists
like Leadbelly and John Hurt from which to choose—and they're all
good—so my choices were fairly arbitrary.

Be aware that the complete recorded works of most of the prewar
artists mentioned here are currently available from Document
Records, so if you like Lonnie Johnson enough to want seven CDs
worth of his early material, refer to that extensive catalog.
Meanwhile, if you're new to the work of a particular artist, the items
in this list will give you a good, accessible starting point.

Garfield Akers, *Son House and the Great Delta Blues Singers,*
    Document 5002.
Anthology of American Folk Music (Harry Smith, ed.), Smithsonian
    Folkways 40090.

Kokomo Arnold, *Bottleneck Guitar Trendsetters of the 1930s,* Yazoo 1049.

Barbecue Bob (Robert Hicks), *Chocolate to the Bone,* Yazoo 2005.

Scrapper Blackwell, *The Virtuoso Guitar of Scrapper Blackwell: 1928–34,* Yazoo 1019.

Blind Blake, *Ragtime Guitar's Foremost Fingerpicker,* Yazoo 1068.

Big Bill Broonzy, *The Young Big Bill Broonzy: 1928–35,* Yazoo 1011.

Willie Brown, *Son House and the Great Delta Blues Singers,* Document 5002.

Bob Brozman, *A Truckload of Blues,* Rounder 3119.

Bo Carter, *Greatest Hits 1930–40,* Yazoo 1014.

Reverend Gary Davis, *Blues and Ragtime,* Shanachie 97024.

Delmore Bros., *Brown's Ferry Blues,* County 116.

Blind Boy Fuller, *East Coast Piedmont Style,* Sony/Legacy 46777.

Jesse Fuller, *Favorites,* Original Blues Classics 528.

Paul Geremia, *The Devil's Music,* Red House 127.

John Hammond, *Live,* Rounder 3074.

Alvin Youngblood Hart, *Big Mama's Door,* Sony/OKeh 67543.

Harvey and Copeland, *Old Time Mountain Guitar,* County 3512.

Sol Hoopii, *Master of Hawaiian Guitar,* Rounder 1024/5.

Lightnin' Hopkins, *Very Best of Lightnin' Hopkins,* Rhino 79860.

Son House, *Son House and the Great Delta Blues Singers,* Document 5002.

Joshua (Peg Leg) Howell, *Complete,* Matchbox 2004/5.

Mississippi John Hurt, *Legend,* Rounder 611100.

Papa Charlie Jackson, *Complete,* Document 5087.

John Jackson, *Front Porch Blues,* Alligator 4867.

Nehemiah (Skip) James, *Complete 1931,* Document 5005.

Lemon Jefferson, *Best of Lemon Jefferson,* Yazoo 2057.

Lonnie Johnson, *Steppin' on the Blues,* Sony/Legacy 46221.

Robert Johnson, *The Complete Recordings,* Sony/Legacy 64916.

Tommy Johnson, *1928–30,* Wolf 104.

Blind Willie Johnson, *The Complete Recordings,* Sony/Legacy 52835.

Little Hat Jones, *Texas Blues: 1927–35,* Document 5161.

Leadbelly (Huddie Ledbetter), *In the Shadow of the Gallows Pole,* Rykodisc 1018.

Furry Lewis, *In His Prime: 1927-28*, Yazoo 1050.

Mance Lipscomb, *Texas Songster*, Arhoolie 306.

Sam McGee, *Complete Early Recordings*, Document 8036.

Blind Willie McTell, *The Early Years*, Yazoo 1005.

Memphis Minnie, *Complete*, Vol. 1, Document 5028.

Charley Patton, *King of the Delta Blues*, Yazoo 2001.

Kelly Joe Phelps, *Lead Me On*, Burnside 0015.

Yank Rachell, *Yank Rachell*, Random Chance 2.

Ikey Robinson, *1929-37*, RST 1508.

Jimmie Rodgers, *The Essential Jimmie Rodgers*, RCA 67500.

John (Funny Paper) Smith, *Complete*, Document 6016.

Frank Stokes, *Creator of the Memphis Blues*, Yazoo 1051.

Tampa Red (Hudson Whitaker), *The Guitar Wizard*, Sony/Legacy 53235.

Jimmie Tarlton, *Steel Guitar Rag*, Hightone 2503.

Henry Thomas, *Texas Worried Blues*, Yazoo 1080.

Willard (Ramblin') Thomas, *Ramblin' Thomas and the Dallas Blues Singers: 1928-32*, Document 5107.

Merle Travis, *Folk Songs of the Hills*, Bear Family 15636.

Dave Van Ronk, *From Another Time and Place*, Alcazar 120.

Aaron (T-Bone) Walker, *Texas Blues: 1927-35*, Document 5161.

Willie Walker, *Ragtime Blues Guitar 1927-30*, Document 5062.

Muddy Waters (McKinley Morganfield), *The Complete Plantation Recordings*, MCA 9344.

James (Curley) Weaver, *Complete 1933-35*, Document 5111.

Sylvester Weaver, *Complete 1923-27*, Document 5112.

Casey Bill Weldon, *Bottleneck Guitar Trendsetters of the 1930s*, Yazoo 1049.

Booker (Bukka) White, *The Complete Sessions 1930-40*, Travelin' Man 03.

Geechie Wiley (with Elvie Thomas), *Mississippi Blues*, Document 5157.

Big Joe Williams, *Shake Your Boogie*, Arhoolie 315.

Oscar Woods, *Texas Slide Guitar*, Document 5143.

Record Companies

Arhoolie Records
10341 San Pablo Ave.
El Cerrito, CA 94530
(510) 525-7471
(888) 274-6654 (orders)
fax (510) 525-1204
www.arhoolie.com

Document Records
12 Saint John St.
Whithorn, Newton-Stewart
DG8 8PE Scotland
(44) 1988-500742
fax (44) 1988-500840
www.document-records.com

Sony/Legacy
550 Madison Ave. Floor 17
New York, NY 10022
(212) 833-8000
www.legacyrecordings.com

Yazoo Records
c/o Shanachie Entertainment
13 Laight St., Sixth Floor
New York, NY 10013
(212) 334-0284
www.shanachie.com

Instruction/Performance Videos

Homespun Tapes
PO Box 340
Woodstock, NY 12498
(845) 246-2250
(800) 338-2737
fax (845) 246-5282
www.homespuntapes.com

Stefan Grossman's Guitar
    Workshop
PO Box 802
Sparta, NJ 07871
(973) 729-5544
fax (973) 726-0568
www.guitarvideos.com

Lawrence Cohn, ed., *Nothing But the Blues,* Abbeville.

David Evans, *Big Road Blues,* Da Capo.

Sheldon Harris, *Blues Who's Who,* Da Capo.

Alan Lomax, *The Land Where the Blues Began,* Pantheon.

Giles Oakley, *The Devil's Music,* Harcourt/Brace.

Paul Oliver, *Songsters and Saints,* Cambridge University.

Mike Rowe, *Chicago Breakdown,* Drake.

Elijah Wald, *Josh White: Society Blues,* University of Massachusetts
    Press.

Gayle Dean Wardlow, *Chasin' That Devil Music,* Miller Freeman.

Tom Wheeler, *American Guitars,* Harper Collins.

Charles Wolfe and Kip Lornell, *The Life and Legend of Leadbelly,*
    Harper Collins.

Following are several established guitar workshop
programs with a strong orientation toward acoustic
blues music. For an extensive, searchable list of guitar workshops,
with links and specialties, visit www.acousticguitar.com.

Acoustic Blues and Slide Guitar
    Workshops
International Guitar Seminars
PO Box 903, Times Square
    Station
New York, NY 10108
(646) 242-4471
fax (413) 460-2430
info@guitarseminars.com
www.guitarseminars.com
Classes with Bob Brozman,
    Woody Mann, and others in
    the U.S. and Canada.

Augusta Heritage Center
    Blues Week
Davis and Elkins College
100 Campus Drive
Elkins, WV 26241
(304) 637-1209
fax (304) 637-1317
augusta@augustaheritagc.com
www.augustaheritage.com

Centrum's Port Townsend
   Country Blues Workshop
PO Box 1158
Port Townsend, WA 98368-0958
(360) 385-3102
fax (360) 385-2470
lizzy@centrum.org
www.centrum.org

Fur Peace Ranch
PO Box 389
Pomeroy, OH 45769
(740) 992 6228
fax (740) 992-9126
info@furpeaceranch.com
www.furpeaceranch.com
*Classes with Jorma Kaukonen
   and guests.*

Kerrville Roots/Blues Guitar
   Camp
The Kerrville Folk Festival
PO Box 291466
Kerrville, TX 78029
(830) 257-3600
fax (830) 257-8680
info@kerrville-music.com
www.kerrville-music.com
*Classes with Steve James and
   guests.*

National Guitar Workshops
Box 222
Lakeside, CT 06758
(800) 234-6479
fax (860) 567-0374
alicia@guitarworkshop.com
www.guitarworkshop.com

Puget Sound Guitar Workshop
1503 E St.
Bellingham, WA 98225-3007
(360) 647-2979
info@psgw.com
www.psgw.com

The Swannanoa Gathering
   Guitar Week
Warren Wilson College
PO Box 9000
Asheville, NC 28815-9000
(828) 298-3434
fax (828) 299-3326
gathering@warren-wilson.edu
www.swangathering.org

MUSICAL EXAMPLES

A-major scale

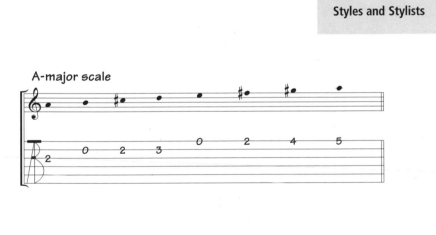

A-major scale with blue notes

12-bar blues

YOU DON'T WANT ME WHY NOT TELL ME SO

YOU DON'T WANT ME WHY NOT TELL ME

SO PACK MY SUIT - CASE

DOWN THE ROAD I'LL GO

Eight-bar blues
"Sitting on Top of the World"

WAS IN THE SPRING ONE SUN - NY DAY MY BA - BY

LEFT ME SHE WENT A - WAY BUT NOW SHE'S GONE AND I DON'T

WOR - RY I'M SIT - TIN' ON TOP OF THE WORLD

Four-beat rhythm

Eight-beat rhythm

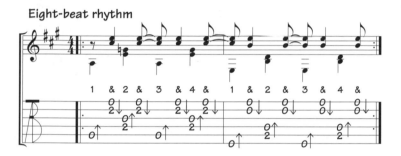

Triplets ("Six over Two")

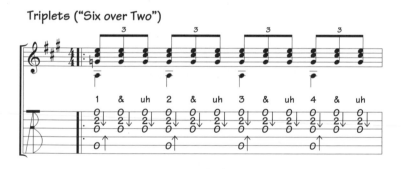

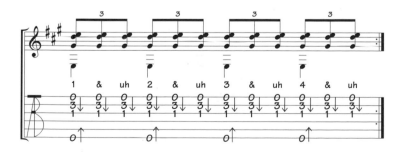

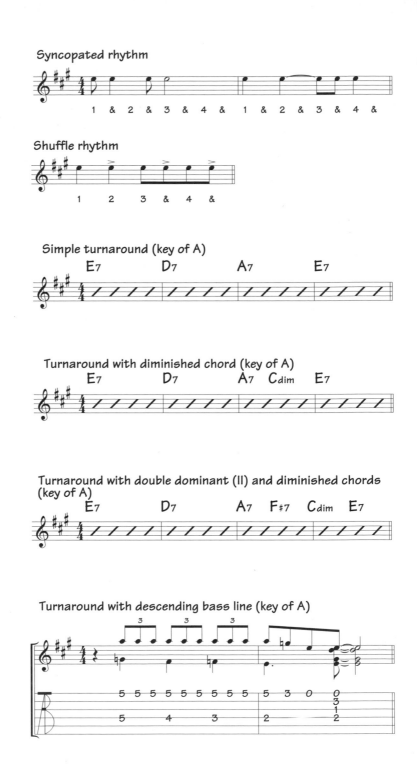

Chromatic scale

Diatonic scale

A-major chord

A7 chord

Steve James

ABOUT THE AUTHOR

Steve James is a touring performer, composer, and multi-instrumentalist based in Austin, Texas. His latest albums include *Boom Chang* on Burnside Records and *Not for Highway Use,* a retrospective compilation on his own Settlement Records. He teaches widely at guitar workshops and clinics and is the author of the CD lesson book *Roots and Blues Fingerstyle Guitar* (String Letter Publishing). For more information, visit his Web site: www.stevejames.com.

OTHER TITLES FROM STRING LETTER PUBLISHING

Roots and Blues Fingerstyle Guitar, by Steve James, $19.95

Part songbook, part oral history lesson, part memoir, this CD–lesson book is a treasure trove of traditional American guitar styles. Learn fingerpicking and slide techniques by playing 25 songs from such roots icons as Furry Lewis, Sam McGee, and Mance Lipscomb, and others.

Acoustic Guitar Slide Basics, by David Hamburger, $16.95

Explore the haunting sounds of acoustic slide guitar and brush up on your bottleneck basics with this easy-to-follow, step-by-step CD–lesson book. Learn the essentials of open tunings and fingerstyle technique, get tips on slide guitars and gear, and more.

Rock Troubadors, by Jeffrey Pepper Rodgers, $14.95

Listen in as today's great rock troubadours share the deeply personal process of nurturing a spark of inspiration into a fully realized piece of music. Includes rare interviews with Paul Simon, James Taylor, Joni Mitchell, Jerry Garcia and David Grisman, Indigo Girls, Chris Whitley, Dave Matthews and Tim Reynolds, Ben Harper, Barenaked Ladies, and Ani DiFranco.

Musical Instrument Auction Price Guide, $39.95

Issued annually, illustrated with full-color plates of noteworthy instruments, the *Auction Price Guide* offers the most comprehensive information available on antique and handmade instrument and bow values. A unique five-year summary, by instrument and maker, of high, low, and average prices shows market trends.

At your music or book store, or order direct • Call (800) 637-2852 • Fax (414) 774-3259 • On-line www.stringletter.com